G000043468

For Clare, Michael, Sarah and a

Eddie (back row, left) with his family on the Headmaster's last
speech day, Old Deanery garden, July 2005

Celebrating Eddie

Howard and Heather Tomlinson

First published in the United Kingdom in 2009
by Howard and Heather Tomlinson

ISBN 978-0-9561862-0-1

Produced by
Action Publishing Technology Limited, Gloucester

Contents

Introduction		1
Chapter 1	Boyhood	5
Chapter 2	After Oxford	18
Chapter 3	Life in Lebanon	32
Chapter 4	Our Via Dolorosa	57
Chapter 5	Home-Coming	65
Chapter 6	Commemorations	75
Chapter 7	Inquest	86
Chapter 8	Grieving	96
Chapter 9	A Faith Challenged	109
Chapter 10	Hanging on to God	119
Chapter 11	Heaven and Healing	129
Chapter 12	The Present and the Future	141

Photographs

We have made every effort to contact the owners of images and gain their approval to reproduce them in this book. The copyright owner of each photograph, except two, is acknowledged in the following list. We have been unable to trace the owners of the copyright of the front cover photograph, taken at St John's College, Oxford, and the image of the young Edward on page 7, taken at Hatch Ride Primary School, Berkshire, but would welcome contact from anyone who could give us any information with regard to the copyright holders of these photographs. The copyright of all images, including our family photographs, is retained by the owner, and may not be copied or used in any other way without prior permission.

[frontispiece] Eddie (back row, left) with his family
   on the Headmaster's last speech day, Old Deanery
   garden, July 2005 (courtesy of Nick Gurgul)   ii
Age 3, with Prudence the cat, summer 1985
(family photograph)   6
A nonchalant 4 year old cricketer, with Michael
   and Sarah, Upcott garden, Wellington College,
   summer 1986 (family photograph)   6
Age 4, taken at Hatch Ride Primary School, November
1985   7
Doing his sums after a day at St James' Primary
   School, *c* 1988 (family photograph)   7
Two brothers together as county captains,
   Wyeside Pavilion, August 1993 (courtesy of the
   Hereford Times)   12

Five scholars (Eddie seated left), Abberley Hall,
c June 1995 (courtesy of Jo Summers)   12

Triumphant school debaters: with Alex Outhwaite,
outside the Old Deanery, Hereford, March 2000
(courtesy of the *Hereford Times*)   16

Smartly dressed as Michael's best man outside St
Weonard's Church, July 2000 (courtesy of Gordon
Taylor)   17

Mr Secretary outside the Oxford Union, May 2003
(family photograph)   19

At the dispatch box of the Oxford Union,
debating for the presidency, summer 2003 (courtesy
of Ed Gallacher)   20

Mr President's celebratory dinner, Macmillan Hall,
December 2003 (family photograph)   20

The President on his landing with his Mum and
Dad, February 2004 (family photograph)   21

Outside 'Schools' after finals, Oxford, June 2005
(courtesy of Richard Bore)   21

Eddie's last rugby match, representing the
Old Herefordians, Wyeside, December 2005
(family photograph)   27

Posing with Michael and niece Esther's lamb,
December 2005 (family photograph)   28

A Beirut Arabic class, University Saint Joseph,
c February 2006 (courtesy of Erwin Julien)   53

Reuben Edward Compton in the capable hands of
Michael Howard and Clare Short, with other
admirers, at the Oxford Union memorial debate,
January 2007 (courtesy of Ed Gallacher)   79

The art of spin bowling: some early cricket coaching
for nephew Ollie, Easter 2004 (family photograph)   146

Nephew Ollie and niece Esther gather with the
rest of the family to celebrate their uncles'
birthdays, October 2005 (family photograph)   146

Back cover photograph by courtesy of John Tiller

Acknowledgements

We are indebted to a number of friends who have encouraged us to write this book, and not least to those who have given us copies of Eddie's letters and emails and/or their own memorial addresses. We would also like to mention Heather Holden-Brown and Sara Maitland, who read and commented on our script; Miles Bailey, who saw the book through the press; our son-in-law, Tim Compton, who allowed us to include his poem, 'Your Uncle Ed'; Lucinda Orr for writing the review; and Chris Poole, who gave us valuable insight into the political situation in Lebanon. For permission to reproduce photographs, we are obliged to Richard Bore, Ed Gallacher, Nick Gurgul, Erwin Julien, Jo Summers, Gordon Taylor, John Tiller and the Editor of the *Hereford Times*.

Since Eddie's death we have been wonderfully supported by our family and many friends, and are particularly grateful for the love and prayers of Val Hamer, Nicholas King, Andrew Law, Michael Tavinor, Paul Towner and the congregations of Hereford Cathedral and St Peter's and St James' Churches, Hereford. But our greatest thanks go to our children, Clare, Michael and Sarah, who have shared – and continue to share – in both our joys and our sorrow, and to whom this book is especially dedicated.

Howard and Heather Tomlinson
Hereford, Epiphany 2009

Note on Eddie's names

Edward rarely used his Christian name in full but generally signed himself 'Eddie' – hence this usage in our title. To some of his friends he was known as 'Ed'; to others 'Eddie' or 'Eddie T'. His family used various permutations on this theme. In this book, therefore – as in his life – we have chosen not to be consistent in our nomenclature. He would have approved.

Introduction

We started this story on 22 July 2006, Day 10 of the Middle East conflict, with the Embassy in Beirut announcing that scheduled evacuations of British citizens from the Lebanon would end the next day. A day or two previously, we had received an email from Erwin, our son Eddie's friend from Toulouse, who told us that he (Erwin) was going to stay behind in Beirut for a few days to try to help the evacuees fleeing in their thousands from the south of Lebanon, just as we feel sure Eddie would have done. Erwin intended to return to France that weekend. Our dear son Eddie, however, was someone who had already been repatriated. He had gone to Beirut, full of ambition and optimism, some nine weeks earlier, to learn Arabic, improve his French and taste the culture of that beleaguered country, but had died, aged 24, of carbon monoxide poisoning from the fumes of a faulty gas heater, on 5 April 2006.

We wrote *Celebrating Eddie* not only as a memorial to a gifted and engaging young man whose sparkling promise was tragically cut short, but also in gratitude to God for the life of a much loved and deeply loving son, brother, uncle and friend; and in the belief that, as is written in the Book of Wisdom (and on Eddie's grave-stone) that the fullness of a man's life is not measured simply by the longevity of his days. Or, as Martin Luther King so prophetically declaimed, longevity only has its place.

If we have been able to recapture something of the affection and warmth of this remarkable young person, who had already achieved so much in his short life but whose real contribution to the world was that (as one of his friends wrote) 'he sought people out and made their day', we will be satisfied. And through the sharing of our grief at his loss, we further hope that we may be able to reflect a little of God's love that has been shown to us in the darkest days of our lives.

The Star

On a clear night
I scan the sky,
Spot the brightest star
And say, 'Hi Ed!'

The star twinkles back.
It seems to draw near
To give me a smile
And say, 'Hi Mum!'

I have not gone mad –
I know that this star
Is not really Ed
And Ed's not the star.

The star's just a symbol
A symbol for Ed,
For while Ed was with us
Ed was a star.

And so
On a clear night
I scan the sky
Pick out the brightest star
And say, 'Hi Ed!

12 February 2008

Chapter 1

Boyhood

In writing this memoir of Edward, it seems important to set the scene by saying something about him as a child, but this is not the place for a blow by blow chronology nor even a series of reminiscences and anecdotes about his devotion to his hamsters or how quickly he learnt his times tables. There is a dictum attributed to the Jesuits, which says 'Give me the child until he is seven and I will show you the man', and that approach seems much more appropriate. Many of the characteristics we saw displayed in Ed's teenage and adult life were clearly sketched in from his earliest days. The problem is where to begin and where to end when there is so much which could be said.

One excellent view of Eddie as a little lad is to be gathered by looking at the montage of photos we prepared for his funeral. There we see young Ed, holding on tight to a full-size rugby ball; or racing down the bank of our Upcott garden on his little red and blue bike; or with his siblings, clutching an ice-cream or giving us the 'thumbs-up'; or with huge cricket gloves dangling off the end of his arms, his left one slung casually over big brother Michael's shoulder. There is one of his head poking out of the top of a tree, startling an unseen Wellington College Speech Day visitor, and another of the industrious child working on some sums at the kitchen table. We can see him having a ride on his brother's shoulders or turning a skipping rope for his sister, or standing beside his little snowman. Often he's stroking a cat. Here is a happy little boy, secure in his family, comfortable in his own skin and always ready for action.

To go back even further it is worth mentioning that Ed's birth was not without incident as he was in the breech position, sitting up cross-legged in his mother's womb. Indeed, it was in this position that, at six months gestation, he spent

Age 3, with Prudence the cat, summer 1985

A nonchalant 4 year old cricketer, with Michael and Sarah, Upcott garden, Wellington College, summer 1986

Age 4, taken at Hatch
Ride Primary School,
November 1985

Doing his sums after a
day at St James' Primary
School, *c* 1988

his first week at St John's College, Oxford, where he was
later to spend his five action-packed university years. For in
the summer of 1981, Howard and I were enjoying the priv-
ilege of vacation study leave at St John's, and in later years

we were able to show him where he had first 'sat' as I
studied. In today's both more cautious and litigious days Ed
would not have been allowed to be born naturally. As it
was, he failed to breathe on arrival and alarm bells were
sounded to summon the emergency team. I am sure that it
was the rapid appearance of this awesome posse of young
men as they stormed into the delivery room which inspired
Ed to start breathing. No way did he want their less than
gentle methods of encouragement.

Nor was his rather traumatic birth the end of his medical
complications, for at six weeks our GP picked up a murmur
in his heart and further tests showed that he had been born
with a hole in his heart. We were warned that side-effects
from this condition could include stunted growth and
limited or slower mental development. These clearly were
not to prove the case for Eddie, but we were worried
enough at the time and our anxiety levels were raised periodically, preceding the various hospital appointments which
were to follow. By the age of four it was clear that Ed's hole
was mending itself and that he was in no way diminished in
size or intelligence.

The next alarm was not until Ed reached the age of
ten. Then, on holiday in Cornwall, he picked up a life-
threatening virus, undiagnosed by a series of three locum
GPs who came to see him in our holiday flat. Eventually, in
a state of deepening anxiety, Howard carried him into the
doctor's surgery in his arms, where he lay limp limbs
dangling, emitting a pathetic little choking cough. At this
point he was rushed to hospital where tests were performed
for every childhood condition that could be imagined – all
to no avail. The doctors were stumped. Eventually they
decided to pump him full of antibiotics, although they were
not confident that this would help as they knew it was a
virus not an infection which was attacking him. But the
regime did work. After the most desperately worrying week,
he began to improve and after a further ten days, he was
allowed to leave hospital once more – to his intense relief.
Ed did not enjoy his stay.

Nor did he enjoy his next hospital stay which he timed very badly to coincide with our twenty-fifth wedding anniversary in 1995. Clare, the eldest of our four children, had arranged a lovely romantic weekend for Howard and me in Malvern, with candle-lit supper and evening concert to set the tone on the Friday, and to end with a surprise party back home in Harley Court on the Sunday. We had left Eddie a bit under the weather, but again a GP had visited and declared it nothing more than a tummy bug, so with his sisters Sarah and Clare uttering reassurances that they could cope, off we went.

It was as well that the weather was wonderful for our Friday evening and that we were able to enjoy the first part of the carefully planned weekend, for at 6am on the Saturday, Clare had had to ring the B and B where we were staying to say that Ed was about to be rushed into hospital with suspected appendicitis. We jumped in the car and drove straight back to spend a worrying day watching over him as he deteriorated in condition. It was a bank holiday weekend and there was only one anaesthetist on duty, and his hands were well and truly full with the results of a road traffic accident. Ed's appendix did not totally burst, but it slowly leaked toxins into his body and he was in a truly pitiful condition by the time he was eventually taken into theatre and operated on. All was well, and Ed made a good recovery, pleading to be let out sooner than he should have been, just to escape the hospital atmosphere. A few weeks later he was down at Wyeside, opening up his scar just a little bit, by joining in the rugby training and tackling the master-in-charge – typical of our 'up and at them' Eddie.

But this is to jump ahead of the story, and I want to return to Eddie's very young days. Ed's arrival had completed the family of four children that Howard and I had always wanted. He slotted readily and easily into the total chaos which was life in a very young family – Clare, our eldest, was exactly five and a half when Ed was born; Michael was four and Sarah was two and a half. In no time at all he was being vigorously bounced in the baby-bouncer, heavily sat on while

lying on his changing mat, enthusiastically splashed in the
bath, and generally welcomed into the family. As soon as he
was able, he sat propped up in his pram amidst the play and
squabbles of his siblings and just watched. I could almost
sense him taking in every detail and recording it for future
reference: he would know exactly what to do once he was old
enough to be out of the pram and in the thick of the action.
And that was where he was to remain for the whole of his
too-short life – in the thick of the action.

Eddie was an easy mixer from the start. In the September
before his birth I had begun teaching one set of lower sixth
pupils for just four 40 minute periods a week. Ed had to fit
into this routine in a variety of ways which were somewhat
unpredictable and *ad hoc*. Often he would be parked in his
pram in a neighbour's garden; occasionally he would come
to the classroom with me; sometimes a friend would have
him. In time, a number of Wellington College wives worked
out a system of mutual child-care as more of us became
involved in similar small-scale forays into the classroom.
Eddie would play happily with whoever was there in our
informal crèche and never seemed to mind the change of
playmate or adult in charge. This ability to be contented in
any company was another characteristic which was readily
recognisable in Ed's later life.

While appearing to be totally malleable and easy-going,
Eddie also had a very independent streak and was not to be
shifted from his chosen path. This manifested itself early on
when he would tire of being bossed around, usually by his
big sister Clare, and would simply amble off rather than do
what she wanted. There is a story elsewhere in this memoir
about Ed often spoiling Clare's dramatic productions by
such behaviour, but this could happen in any situation. Ed
was non-confrontational in approach: unlike the other
siblings, he would not quarrel or argue, he just wandered
off, and no amount of persuasion or coercion would bring
him back. It was totally infuriating!

I can remember only one occasion where I persuaded
Eddie to follow my suggested course of action rather than

his, and that was over his choice of German instead of Spanish for his second modern language. I was proved to be wrong. Eddie never enjoyed German and felt cross that he had not followed his instinct to stick to a Latin based language. If anything, this confirmed Ed in his conviction that he should always listen to advice, then do exactly what he wanted.

So early on in his life Eddie showed that he could be both easy-going, yet firmly independent. Similarly we could see in the young Ed both his forward planning and his total lack of urgency here and now. On moving to Hereford at the age of nearly six, he attended St James' Church of England Primary School, while Michael went to Abberley Hall, a preparatory school near Worcester. On noticing how tatty his school satchel had become – undoubtedly handed down from Michael or Clare – I promised Ed a new one on his sixth birthday in the coming October. Ed's reply was, 'Do you think it will be worth it, Mummy? I shall be going to Abberley in two year's time.' At that point he had been to Abberley on just a few Saturdays to watch Michael playing rugby and had evidently already decided that he would follow in his brother's foot-steps as soon as he could, as indeed he did, two years later. This was not necessarily our intention for Ed back in 1987, but he was already planning his future.

Once at Abberley, Ed worked his way into the scholarship set in order to learn Greek, and from Hereford Cathedral School, he employed much research and military precision, to achieve his entry into Oxford. Once at Oxford, he carefully calculated his route into the rooms he wanted to occupy in his third and fourth years, and, of course, he employed all manner of means to gain his positions as President of both the University Conservative Association and the Union. It is strange to recollect that this aspect of his personality was already clearly evident in the little lad of five.

At the same time as the not quite six year old Eddie was mapping out his move to Abberley, actually getting him to his primary school on time was a daily challenge. This was

Two brothers together as county captains, Wyeside Pavilion,
August 1993

Five scholars (Eddie seated left), Abberley Hall, *c* June 1995

not at all because he was unhappy there: on the contrary, he loved it. The problem was that he had no sense of time passing. After breakfast he would be sent upstairs to clean his teeth. Sarah, who also attended St James', could accomplish this without hitch, and the two of us would grow ever more impatient as Ed failed to reappear. The usual cause for delay was his discovery on the stairs of one of the cats, which he would then sit and stroke at great length, with great tenderness, totally unaware of the ticking away of the minutes. The same could occur when he trotted off to find his shoes or PE kit, or indeed anything at all. Those who have waited a very long time for Ed to put in a promised appearance will no doubt recognise this particular foible. In fairness to Felix and Mittens, I feel that it was not the cats that caused his lateness but Ed's pleasure in each moment which made him incapable of hurrying it along. In the daily rush and stress which too frequently marks much of life today, I cannot help feeling that Ed had a point. The problem was that his relaxed approach made everyone else's life more rushed and stressful.

Another characteristic feature of Ed's later life which manifested itself early on was his lack of materialism. Ed rarely had much that was new. Most of his clothes and toys were handed down and passed on from the older siblings and Ed expected nothing different. He rarely asked for anything and, in common with the rest of the family, would accept 'no' for an answer. The various fads and crazes for collecting this or that seemed to pass him by, and he felt no need at all to possess the 'must have' toy of the moment. When he was a bit older and going out to buy his own clothes, he would happily buy the special offers, such as 'one pair of jeans for ten pounds: two for fifteen'. Various girl friends tried to raise his standards and improve his sartorial sense, but to no avail. To Ed, it just did not matter.

This is not to suggest that later on Ed had no interest in clothes at all. When buying a suit for the sixth form at school, he spent a very long time choosing the one he wanted, as indeed he did when buying another for his work-experience placements in the summer of 2005. He was also very pleased to be given the tuxedo jacket bought for and rejected by Michael one Christmas, and when attending formal dinners or functions, he could brush up smartly and look the part. Indeed he packed DJ and all the trimmings for Beirut, just in the unlikely case they were needed, but he counter-balanced this by also taking out well-worn shoes which developed holes and let in water within a very short time of his arrival. (Note again the contrast in his short-term and long-term planning.) Ed would not have dreamt of following the Gordon Brown example of refusing to wear a dinner suit to a Mansion House dinner, but when the occasion did not require a special mode of dress, he would usually be in flip-flops, baggy tracksuit bottoms and rugby-shirt, or shorts and T-shirt. For Ed neither judged people nor expected to be judged by what he possessed or wore.

Despite his later joking protestations that he suffered greatly from being the youngest of four, in reality his position in the family gave him every advantage. He did not have the responsibilities of the oldest child, nor the striving for position of the middle ones. This, I am sure, helped reinforce Ed's generally buoyant nature. He was a cheerful little chap, good company, eager to learn about the world, and he had three older siblings keen to teach him and show him the way. It would not be until his teens and the stress of public exams that the occasional 'Eyeore' moods set in, and all was woe, woe and thrice woe for a while.

No description of the young Eddie, brief as this must be, can be complete without an acknowledgement of the Christian input into his life. Not only did it influence his approach to living, but the way he embraced it reveals many insights into the personality of the adult Ed: his enthusiasm, his communication skills, his unquenchable optimism and his quiet assurance.

Eddie had been conceived soon after my own faith came to life and from his earliest weeks he was taken to church on Sundays, and he attended Sunday school, when he was three. The Easter when he was three and a half years old, the Sunday school teacher had evidently told the children the story of the resurrection – a daunting challenge to get over to such young children, but one at which she had clearly excelled. Eddie joined us back in the church eyes wide with excitement at the wonderful message. He gabbled his way through the story at break-neck speed and with wonderful simplicity he summed it up in the words immortalized in our family folk-lore, 'Where's de body?' Already he was grabbed by the mystery: his enthusiasm for it never wavered.

From the age of five or six, he joined with our older children at bed-time, in using the Scripture Union bible study notes called, 'Quest'. These were brilliant and Ed gained a fantastic bible grounding from them. The editors, one of whom was called Mary, often invited her readers to write in response to whatever they had read. Eddie, already the great communicator that his friends and family were later to know and love, needed no further bidding to pick up his pencil and scribble something off, and the letters between them became a regular occurrence. I used to wonder whether Mary's heart sank at receiving yet another missive from Ed, but knowing how much joy and pleasure Ed's letters and emails were to bring to us all in later years, I now suspect that her face broke into a smile when she recognised the familiar writing on the envelope.

Eddie did nothing by halves and he wanted to carry on his bed-time routine when he started at boarding school. How, we wondered, would bible reading go down with the rest of the dormitory? The wild optimism which was so much a feature of Ed's later life was already evident in him at the age of eight. He thought that once the other boys saw how great the Quest notes were they would be joining him in reading them. Every term he returned to school with half a dozen spare copies for anyone who might want them, but nobody ever did. Ed was sufficiently his own man, however, not to be daunted by this: he carried on reading his bible and, as far as we knew, he was never teased for this eccentricity.

It is difficult at this distance and in these circumstances, not to write a panegyric rather than a realistic account of the young Ed. Like all children, he had his moments, and the ups and downs of ordinary life beset him just as they do everyone else, but he was a relatively easy child to bring up. He had a cheerful outlook on life, a quiet confidence, and he recognised that he had been blessed with many gifts and was determined to make the most of them. He saw life as an adventure to be lived to the full, from learning to abseil and paddle a kayak on a Christian holiday camp at the age of nine, to parachute jumping at the age of sixteen, to taking himself off to Beirut for a post degree gap year at the age of twenty-four. We deeply wish with all our hearts that the ending could have been different, but there is precious little else in Ed's story that we would ever have wanted to alter ... and we had no say in the ending.

Triumphant school debaters: with Alex Outhwaite, outside the Old Deanery, Hereford, March 2000

Smartly dressed as Michael's best man outside St Weonard's
Church, July 2000

Chapter 2

After Oxford

We never quite understood why Eddie had wanted to learn Arabic. After all, he certainly did not need another language on his cv to convince any future employer that he was a good linguist. Following his four year degree course in *Literae Humaniores* at Oxford, on top of about ten more learning Greek and Latin at school, his command of the classical languages was more than competent; and although he had not studied French for some five years, he had gained a distinction in his 'A' level French – to match his A grades on the other papers – so did he really need to live in a French speaking country for a few months, as he claimed, to scrape away the rust? In any case, he had finally made up his mind to follow his brother into the Law, and fluency in French and Arabic was not an obvious prerequisite for a career at the Bar.

In fact, Ed did not need too much more on his cv at all. Although he did not get – and given all the time he had spent on his political and sporting pursuits, hardly deserved – a 'first', his 2.1 was satisfactory enough (not, incidentally, that Ed thought so), and more than compensated for by an array of other honours and achievements during his five years at the university.

Indeed, as Jonathan McDonagh, one of his friends later observed at the St. John's memorial service:

> Nobody who met Eddie could fail to be impressed by him. It seems that whatever could be mentioned in a university prospectus, Eddie had done and what's more excelled in. In sport, he represented university and college cricket and rugby teams; he was a member of countless societies; and, of course when it came to student politics, he was a colossus, becoming president of OUCA and of the Union. He was a champion debater and known throughout the university for his charisma. There is no doubt that he had conquered Oxford and got out of it pretty much as was humanly possible.

Jonathan had also added that Eddie had enjoyed other extra-mural pursuits while at Oxford. One was roof-

Mr Secretary outside the Oxford Union, May 2003

At the dispatch box of the Oxford Union, debating for the
presidency, summer 2003

Mr President's celebratory dinner, Macmillan Hall, December
2003

The President on his landing with his Mum and Dad,
February 2004

Outside 'Schools' after finals, Oxford, June 2005

climbing around the colleges, his favourite perch apparently being just behind Charles I's statue in Canterbury
quad in his own college – an attic room of which Ed had
secured, by ballot, after a carefully planned campaign. By
the time Eddie had revealed his regal hide-away to his
friend (in 2003-04), Ed had (in Jon's words) 'won all the
elections he would ever need to win at Oxford and he sat
there as if on his very own throne looking out over the
city.' It was as well that we did not know that Eddie had
tried 'to notch up' as many college roof-tops as he could
during his under-graduate career (rather, I assume, as Scot-
tish fell-walkers bag 'munros'). However, we could not
help learning about his roof-climbing exploits at the Union,
as he had fallen through a plate-glass sky-light there during
his presidential sabbatical, and had spent that summer
holiday at home, in enforced study, resting his 50 stitched
leg. The injury put an end to his university rugby career
but may have saved his degree.

Unsurprisingly, Eddie did not draw attention to these
climbing conquests on his cv, although he did mention that
he had 'successfully negotiated parachute training while at
school.' However, he was not afraid to admit on his resumé
that in 2003 he had been a co-founder member of a discussion and dining society, 'the Ratcatchers' – a poor man's
'Bullingdon', I suspect, but possibly more civilised and a
club of which Ed was sufficiently proud to use an image of
its membership as his screen-saver. To have a photograph of
your friends prominently displayed on your computer was
one thing, but to include them on your cv was perhaps
taking a bit of a risk. But that was Eddie. He was confident
and optimistic and a calculated risk-taker throughout his
life and, through hard work, as well as foresight and good
judgement, these risks had generally paid off handsomely.

It was safer for Eddie to have acknowledged on his cv that
he was a chapel warden at St John's, and had helped 'with
the running of the chapel, organising and taking readings,
intercessions, short evening services and charity events'.
This was entirely truthful but not quite the whole story. A

series of e-mails with the chaplain Liz Carmichael, suggest that Eddie was not the most reliable chapel monitor ever appointed to that role, and that sometimes 'the conflicting demands of his diary' (as Fr Nick King later so nicely put it) got the better of him. Still, he recognised his own short-comings. Having missed the Sunday Evensong at which Fr Nick had preached, he left a message on the chaplain's answer phone – albeit a rather incoherent one – and then emailed her at 3.21 am on the morning of 25 November 2002: 'something went horribly wrong with my timings this evening ... I am furious with myself for this ... I am a fan of his and I feel my non-appearance tonight and this lack of support has let him down. aaarrrrg. I just don't know what came over me.' After gentle chastisement, Ed was forgiven. Some years later the chaplain reflected: 'Ed was very nice to have around ... He led prayers well ... the problem was quite often that he operated on a different time-table!' – that and (in Liz's words) 'his delightful insouciance', as he read the lesson in shorts and flip-flops at a smart 'gaudy' for old college members.

His cv may not have told the whole truth but it was sufficiently impressive – allied, no doubt to the charm, intelligence and knowledge he had shown at interview – to have persuaded his interviewers at the Middle Temple, towards the end of his time at Oxford, to grant him an Astbury scholarship and Harmsworth exhibition. These awards would have gone a long way towards financing his law studies. So why did he need to delay taking up these scholarships and embarking on his law conversion course, for which he had paid a sizeable deposit, by spending a year learning Arabic, thereby necessitating a postgraduate gap year?

As usual, Eddie approached his parents circumspectly and was not wholly forthcoming in his explanation to them. Loving and giving as he was, he could treat his family on a 'need to know' basis, as was the case in this instance. Never-theless, we did discuss it and, as I remember, a key part of his argument was that after his particularly strenuous final year at Oxford, if he did not take another year out, he might flunk the law course. In any case, he stressed, this was a year out but not a year off, and learning Arabic and improving his French could only enhance his future prospects. As Ed later explained to his former prep school Headmaster (in response to a communication of mine the previous year) in an email which was published posthumously in the *Old Abberley News*:

> I have now learned the lesson that it is best to send you news personally, rather than allow my father the opportunity of putting spin on my own affairs. I see from [the 2005 edition] ... that I have 'finally' completed my degree at Oxford – when I was only one year behind schedule, and for a rather good reason, too!!!!! [Owing to his election as President of the Oxford Union, Ed had taken a year out between the third and fourth years of his degree.] It also seems unfair for him to describe me as having 'another GAP' – when I hadn't taken one before Oxford, only one (unscheduled) in the middle ... In fact, I'm hardly Gap-ing in the sense of bumming around on a Queensland beach or driving around the US like an 18 year old. Humph!

And what did it matter that he would be a year or two older than many of his contemporaries when seeking pupillage?

As the above retort shows, there was no real meeting of minds over this. Nevertheless, we respected his arguments. And, in the end, we left it that if he could persuade the Middle Temple and the law college to defer the scholarships and transfer the deposit to the following academic year, we would go along with his plan. Perhaps we should have tried harder to persuade him otherwise. In retrospect, I sometimes think that I should have brought 'the power of the purse' to bear on his decision. But that was not our way. Moreover, Ed could be incredibly stubborn once his mind was made up, and, at 23, was well beyond the stage of being influenced by parental persuasion of this kind. And who could either gainsay his Oxford achievements or question the value of a productive post-degree 'gap', prior to Ed's intended career in public law and then later – if the cards had fallen – in national politics as (in the words of a friend) 'a sensible moderate Tory'?

Once he had secured the necessary consent, Ed engaged on his preparations for his time abroad, from our Hereford home, with his customary determination and enthusiasm. For the first time in almost 20 years, he had come to the beginning of an academic year without being tied to the frame-work of an educational institution. Despite the freedom which this independence had given him, his hectic life at university had taught him – or was this an innate skill? – how he could effectively juggle many different tasks simultaneously, with only the occasional missed catch. He was particularly concerned both to improve his French and start learning Arabic, and he organised public and private languages classes to that end. His advanced French conversation class proved useful in rolling back the years since 'A' level, even though most of his class-mates were his senior by some forty years. One later remembered how she and Ed had 'enjoyed bouncing not quite fluent conversations off each other'. Learning Arabic, inevitably, proved to be more challenging.

Two things now strike me as I now look through Ed's Arabic text books and notes. First, it becomes clearer from this first paragraph of *Introduction to Arabic Letters and Sounds*, why Eddie wanted to learn Arabic:

> The beauty of the Arabic language, both spoken and written
> – and the richness of the Arabic-speaking world, its history
> and culture – has recently become of increasing importance
> and a matter of revelation for the English-speaking world. It
> is essential as this new century unfolds that understanding
> develops between nations – and language is the magic key.

And second, as I go through his file, I am impressed by the thoroughness with which he undertook the task of learning a new language. Eddie was a fanatical grammarian, and this is quite evident from the detailed lists of Arabic numbers, ordinals, vocabulary and phrases (for example, 'hello and welcome', 'where are you from?', 'I am from Hereford', 'I studied at Oxford', 'I am 24 years old' and – appropriately – 'sorry I'm late!') that he had compiled. Not that we could help him much with the language, but Heather did her best to imitate the sounds from the tape so that she could test Eddie in the evening on the Arabic phrases that he had learned that day. The Arabic for 'computer' (pronounced 'kumbyootorrr') became something of a family joke and was my sole contribution to Ed's mastery of Arabic. Heather also baked a cake to commemorate Ed's 24th birthday on 26 October 2005, iced with the words transliterated into Arabic script, 'Habby Birthday' because there are no p's in Arabic. He appreciated that.

There was also the rather more mundane question of Eddie earning sufficient money to finance the trip abroad. This was a new experience for Eddie. He had been in the privileged position of not having to finance himself through university and he did not have any student debts (a small loan apart) to pay off, so that anything he earned after his degree could be put aside for his travels. In the summer he had undertaken unpaid mini-pupillages and a short, well remunerated, vacation stint with the commercial law firm, SJ Berwin, where he had apparently made an impression, as we later discovered, showing 'an interest in everyone he met' and 'a charming, self-deprecating manner, which put people at their ease'. But this was not sufficient to fund his gap project so he took two jobs in Hereford which meant he could live at home. The first was as a temporary secretary in a local solicitors' office, a job which (pettily as it now seems) we made him start straight away, rather than delay for a couple of weeks, which meant that he had to forfeit his (rather furtively) planned Portuguese holiday with his friends. Anyone less secretary-like than Edward could scarcely be imagined. Indeed, for his Union work he some-times seemed to have relied more on my PA than on his own secretarial skills. Nevertheless, although not always effi-cient – 'he wasn't perfect and opened a few of my files upside down', one partner was to remember – he was always welcoming and made time for people. The same solicitor later admitted that 'it was a mark of Ed's personality that I always wanted to find time to stop and talk to him'. And the front of house nature of the post did give Ed time to read the broadsheets on a daily basis, as was his wont in the holidays. His second temporary post was the usual student fall-back of bar-man at a local restaurant, which paid better but meant longer and less sociable hours. In consequence, we saw much less of him over Christmas 2005 than we or his siblings would have liked. Still, he confided in us that black-currant juice and soda was the best value drink in the establishment, a tipple which has become our own particular favourite at that place.

Eddie's last rugby match, representing the Old Herefordians, Wyeside, December 2005

Posing with Michael and niece Esther's lamb,
December 2005

Meanwhile, Eddie was planning his 'little adventure'
overseas, as he put it. Although he was not particularly well
travelled, aside from family holidays and school visits
abroad, he had seen something of both America – having
toured the States during two Union debating tours – and the
classical sites (and beaches) of Greece. But he had never
been to those former French colonies bordering the south-
ern and eastern Mediterranean where Arabic, as well as
French, was the *lingua franca*. That such countries had
bordered the ancient classical worlds, and also held the
remains of archaeological sites of considerable antiquity
and interest, was a further incentive to go there, as perhaps
was the fact that a few of them were politically unstable.
Indeed, as someone who had contributed occasional
columns for student newspapers during his time at Oxford

('Dinners with Eddie' being one such feature), and who hoped to file a story or two to the nationals from North Africa or the Middle East, the political turbulence of these regions was very likely an added bonus.

Eddie had originally intended to go to Tunisia. As he explained in one of his many letters seeking employment in that country: 'De janvier 2006, j'espères habiter en Tunisie pendant six mois au moins avec une famille locale, pour améliorer mon Français et mon Arabe, pour voir les sites anciennes, et pour faire l'expérience de la vie à l'étranger'. He may also have had an academic interest in the country, having probably read something about its history for his 'A' level history project on the kingdom of Sicily in the twelfth century, when that part of the north African coast was held for a time by the Normans; and for his Ancient History degree papers, he was likely to have done some research on Carthage during its seven century rule by Rome. We do not quite know. But his choice made good sense to us. As a former French protectorate, Tunisia fulfilled his language criteria – in spite of a vernacular Tuscan Arabic being the common spoken dialect. Moreover, the standard of living there was among the best in the developing world; and the country seemed relatively stable politically, a point under-lined by the visit our daughter-in-law had made to Tunisia as few years earlier as part of her undergraduate course. Frances had even lent Eddie her tourist guide to the country. Had we then realised the severe restrictions imposed even on western journalists when writing on Tunisian soil – and knowing as we did Ed's intentions to write – we would have been less happy.

Eddie worked hard over several months trying to estab-lish contacts with Tunisia. For example, he wrote to 'Le Premier Ministère' (Place du Gouvernement, La Kasabah, 1008 Tunis) enquiring whether a suitable placement might be available ('Est-ce-que ce serait possible de travailler chez le bureau de Premier Ministre comme correcteur orthographique pour les fonctionnaires de Ministère?'). Ed believed in going to the top and was nothing if not

optimistic! He also tried to exploit Oxford contacts, as well
as my one link with the diplomatic service. As late as 11
January 2006, less than three weeks before his eventual
departure, he wrote to a friend of a friend 'to see if you have
any employment opportunities or recommendations for my
time in the Arab world'. This letter makes it perfectly clear
that he was still intent on going to Tunisia, but time was
getting short, and despite all his efforts nothing seemed to
be working out – either with regard to the prospect of
employment or seeking suitable accommodation or
enrolling on an Arabic course at a university. Doors kept
opening a little, and then were repeatedly slammed shut in
his face. It was an immensely frustrating time for him.

    And then, within a matter of days, a Lebanese door
opened and remained so, the key strangely being provided
by the Patriarch of Antioch, a guest of the Union during
Eddie's student days, and the Oxford Maronites, who gave
him the necessary introductions. Lebanon had always been
in the back of his mind as a possible base. On 7 October, he
had heard from a London friend about the possibilities of
an English student getting work as a copy editor on the
Lebanese *Daily Star* and other English journals. Two days
later, Ed had replied: 'Thanks for the Lebanon update – very
encouraging indeed! Will be sure to email the *Daily Star*
promptly. I can only assume, however, that the tone is somewhat dissimilar from fair Albion's own daily of the same
name?' But it was not until mid January, after his Tunisian
contacts had dried up, that he finally settled on Lebanon,
following the offer of accommodation at the Maronite
Catholic university in Jounieh, some 20 kilometres to the
north of Beirut, and his application and acceptance on an
Arabic course at St Joseph's University. On 25 January Ed
arranged a new (and more expensive) travel insurance
package to Lebanon, which included cover for trips to Syria
and Jordan, and over the next few days he made his final
preparations – ordering his Lebanese currency, arranging
for a banking deposit account in Beirut, and – having
bought a new and suitably coloured suitcase – packing. In a

final whirl-wind weekend, he travelled to London to say good-bye to his friends, while we arranged the final banking details with Lloyds, returning home late on the Monday, the day before his departure, just in time to sign the money transfer.

We had little time to react to this change of plan. It is true that we were not entirely happy about his going to Lebanon, not least because of its troubled recent history. But the fact that the jigsaw had fallen into place so quickly was reassuring, as was the chance discovery of a further contact – a former pupil of Hereford Cathedral School, where I had been Headmaster, was now a business-man in Beirut. Ian had promised to meet Ed at the airport and give him over-night accommodation before taking him to the monastic residence in Jounieh. It all seemed propitious, if not providential.

Although the crucial detail still eludes me, I can recall many moments of Tuesday 31 January 2006, that last day with Eddie, the day I drove him to Heathrow – the last minute packing and weighing of suitcases; the stop for petrol off the A 417; the difficulty of finding parking at Terminal 4; his insistence on buying drinks at the pre-departure lounge, while waiting for his flight, so that we had a legitimate claim to eating our packed lunches on the seats provided for the café patrons. My final good-bye – the last time I was to see Eddie alive – was, as it seems to me now, perfunctory and, in retrospect, not what it should have been. I did not even give him a proper hug – simply shaking hands and putting a fatherly arm around his broad shoulders. 'Take care', I may have said. We then both took our leaves. Was there a backward glance and a final wave? How I wish that I could remember.

Chapter 3

Life in Lebanon

Had Ed been of an earlier generation, and had the centre still existed, he would have been far better suited to learning Arabic at the Middle East Centre for Arabic Studies at Shemlan – that institution in the Lebanese hills founded by the British government in 1947 that became renowned as a spy school and one of the best places to learn Arabic in the world. Nevertheless, despite the qualms of his parents and some of his friends, from Eddie's view-point, Lebanon in 2006 was not a bad place to spend a few months.

The Université Saint-Joseph, a late nineteenth century Jesuit foundation, was well recognised and offered him a suitable introductory Arabic course. Moreover, as the first francophone university to open in Lebanon, and unlike the equally well established American University of Beirut, it was primarily a French-speaking institution which again suited Ed's purposes. Indeed, as a former mandated territory, French remained the second language of the country and was taught (with Arabic) as a compulsory language throughout the twelve years of a Lebanese school curriculum. And French influence remained strong, not least among Lebanese Christian communities which still comprised a sizeable minority of the population.

Historically, too, there was plenty to interest Ed in a country that went back over 5000 years. Originally home to the Phoenicians, and then subsequently occupied by the

Assyrians, the Persians, the Greeks, the Romans, the Arabs and the Ottoman Turks – as well as the French – Lebanon abounded in archaeological sites from classical antiquity. As a classicist and potential jurist, he may have been aware that in Roman times Beirut's school of law was one of the earliest and most influential law schools of that empire; as someone with a keen biblical knowledge, he would have known some of the references in the Psalms and the Song of Songs to the cedars of Lebanon, even if he could not have placed all 71 of them; and as a Christian, he would have realised that Beirut was the most Christian capital in the Middle East.

It was just that Eddie had not arrived at quite the right time. Had he been able to come to Lebanon a few years earlier, he would have found a country that was relatively stable politically and one recovering economically from the disastrous wars of 1975-90, even if not to the extent of the 1960s, when Beirut was known as the Paris of the Middle East. The assassination of Prime Minister Rafik Hariri in a car bomb explosion on 14 February 2005, however, had changed the political climate – marking the beginning of a series of further assassination attempts against prominent Lebanese politicians, and sparking the 'cedar revolution' and the subsequent withdrawal of Syrian troops from Lebanon. At the beginning of 2005, there had been a degree of optimism about the future of a country which was slowly resolving its difficulties; a year later, when Ed arrived, it was a time of considerable tension and uncertainty. Not that this worried Ed – indeed, it added to his sense of mission and adventure.

As befits a polished wordsmith and fine communicator, Ed was a frequent and amusing correspondent, and during the remaining nine weeks of his life, his activities in Lebanon can be chronicled through his postcards ('posties' as he called them), emails, and – for his first two weeks – a detailed 10,000 word diary which he kept from 4th to 16th February and which we found among his papers after his death. Although we will never quite know why he started it, the last part of his first entry suggests that he regretted not keeping one before:

> I realise how even the very writing of a diary is a totally self-obsessed act, of course. I've never bothered before, but regret that now – especially thinking of my eventful Oxford years. Reading this [entry] again, I seem rather neurotic, when I'm actually really terribly contented. What a privileged life. I've just got to be honest with this!

However, Ed was never sufficiently self-absorbed, and had never made the time to keep a daily record about his university life. It is a pity, for he was a natural diarist. But we must be content with this wonderful survival of Ed's voice – the intimate journal, kept over a few days, of a gifted young man who was relishing his freedom and both coming to terms with and trying to make sense of a different culture.

After spending the first night in the Middle East at Ian's flat and following enquiries about setting up a bank account at the Banque Audi in Jounieh, Ed was welcomed at the Foyer des Apôtres on the afternoon of Wednesday February 1 by Fr Khalil Ahmed, who had been contacted on Ed's behalf, by Fr Shafiq Abouzayd, a Maronite living in Oxford. Ed's residence – a room within 'the Apostles Dorm' – was (in his own words) 'not exactly de luxe accommodation, but it will certainly do', although he later recorded that there was a strange 'stench' of sewage when he tried to sleep facing on his left side, of which he was never aware when he rolled over on his right shoulder. Apart from the one night, this smell did not worry him unduly. 'My bed is very comfortable indeed', he wrote', 'and generally speaking I have no complaints about my room'. Its real glory was the balcony from which there was a magnificent view. He would spend some time most nights on this perch, looking out over the Lebanese hills and listening to the music he had brought with him on his CD player. He had catholic tastes, as these two diary extracts reveal:

Suitably moved by the end of the Hemmingway, [he had just finished reading *A Farewell to Arms*] I plugged myself in full blast to my favourite *Magic Flute* aria on my personal CD player. I then got cross with myself for not knowing it by name, only by its track number (7...), and for now being almost incapable of singing. I feel I can't do anything really really well, just lots of things reasonably (badly). For example, it would be great to belt out that Mozart aria from my balcony every night before sleep for the appreciative Lebanese masses. Alas, I'll never make it ...

I ended this thoroughly enjoyable day by listening to my personal CD player on my balcony for the first time in a while. I put on the boy-band, slushy CD which I burned at Pete Shutt's in Bristol and which, embarrassingly enough, I totally adore. I happily bopped away for a good 40 minutes to things like Backstreet Boys 'As long as you love me' and Elton John & Blue's 'Sorry seems to be the hardest word'. When James Blunt's 'You're Beautiful' came on, I thought to address it to the monumental statue of the Holy Virgin, illuminated clearly at the top of the steep hillside at Harissa. I wondered whether that was rather blasphemous. Then I thought the last line of 'I will never be with you' perhaps rather appropriate for an Anglican non-Catholic. But then I considered that 'never being with Madonna' might mean I would never get to heaven.

This rather unnecessary mental debate came to a conclusion when Take That's 'Back for Good' came on. I clearly got very excited and started to sing loudly, as at that moment Joseph popped his head out of the window next door. He smiled and the two of us saluted with both our hands the afore mentioned monumental Madonna of Harissa. He probably didn't have the line 'your lipstick marks still on my coffee cup' going through his head though ...

Once on his way back from Beirut, Eddie had fallen into conversation with a Lebanese stranger, who (Ed's diary relates) 'could speak many languages, was very well qualified, was working in the tourist industry here and wanted to work abroad'. Having paid for Ed's bus fare, the business man invited Ed over to dinner to meet his family. Ed willingly gave out his email address but then recorded his reservations:

Two things do worry me, however: will he think I can help
him get his dream ticket to a visa to Britain, and will I be
bombarded by invitations to this, that and the other? I can
imagine that in his enthusiasm and openness and generosity
he would want me to see him all the time. In my British
manner, I will simply want to choose my own friends and my
own moments. We're not good at instant enthusiasm and
friendship.

Despite this perception, Ed had a great gift for friendship,
and he quickly made acquaintances with his fellow residents, even if he found some of the students rather 'juvenile
and materialistic', having perceived that they had mocked
Fahdi, the porter – and in English so that he could not
understand – and had rather sneered at himself for 'walking
round the Foyer in socks and an unkempt state'. He chatted
easily to Foyer staff – to the cleaning lady, with whom he
kept his French going well and who was pleased to hear his
Arabic phrases; to Père Toni, 'a smart 30 something'
Maronite priest in charge of student accommodation; and
to Fahdi himself, as this extract illustrates:

> I have just finished an enjoyable conversation with the
> Foyer's porter Fahdi. He wanted to know about Christianity
> in GB and USA and whether there were many Maronites
> where I came from. He was very surprised when I told him
> that I had never met any before arriving here. Bearing in
> mind that Fahdi was speaking in his third language (Arabic
> 1st, Italian 2nd) that I was speaking in my second and that
> the subject matter was 'the rôle of the cult of saints and the
> Holy Mother of God in worldwide Christianity today', the
> conversation did at times become a little stilted. Fahdi
> seemed genuinely perplexed, even affronted, when I tried to
> explain that Anglicans tended not to pray to the Madonna
> (or the saints) on the grounds that she wasn't divine and that
> only God could forgive sins. 'So when you go to church, you
> don't pray to the Madonna?' 'No, I don't.' 'But if I came
> to your house, you'd expect me to talk to your mother,
> wouldn't you?' I had no comeback to this righteous argu-
> mentation! Fahdi was keen to point out that at a shrine to

Mary in the Bekaa valley there had been thousands of healing miracles and that he knew of Jordanian Muslims who had been healed there too. I had no idea what to say to that, certainly not in French anyway.

Ed's neighbour, Joseph, also proved companionable:

I had an enjoyable dinner with my neighbour here ... I was very pleased to be given free food and to save some pennies. He is a very kind man in his fifties who I think makes icons for a living. His two rooms are extraordinary – packed full of clutter of various types: most obviously 100s of icons and candles, posters and pictures of saints and patriarchs, bedding and food. With a microwave and hob he cooks a lot of his own food. He has a protruding white beard and thick brown glasses, and wears what appear to be baggy pyjamas most of the day. He has the most terrible hacking cough and walks with a sprightly shuffle. He tends to look about a metre above your head when talking to you, which is quite disconcerting. Even more difficult is his habit of chatting to me in Arabic. But by pointing lots and slipping into French now and then we get by. I do feel like I am improving a little.

Having introduced me to the Armenian Church service in French on Sunday, he's taking me to St Antoine's early tomorrow morning for a Maronite mass. That'll mean a relatively early 7.40 start for me, by which time ... [he] would have been awake for almost three hours. [He] ... has reminded me that it is St Maroon's day on Thursday, which I imagine will be a spectacular and exciting occasion. He was very unimpressed by the violent Islamic rioting yesterday, performing for me a few disdainful 'Allahu Akbar's to make his point. That some crucifixes and churches had been attacked made him very upset. At some point I thought he said the rioters would go to hell – although I couldn't be sure.

On other occasions:

Feeling that I had spent too much money recently, I went next door to see Joseph for some supper at 8.15pm. Putting

[it] like that, I'm feeling guilty as if I am just using him for
free food. But Joseph seems to really appreciate the company
and as he doesn't get a lot he enjoys the act of hospitality –
just bumping into him in the corridor he asks me if I want
any food to eat. Our meetings are a strange affair, as he chats
away in Arabic / Syriac and I do my best to follow. I can
actually understand his main thrust most of the time, and he
will slip into French every now and then. The food was very
good, and despite our different languages, cultures and lives,
I really enjoyed the occasion. He promised to come and see
me in the Armenian Church after his Syriac Catholic service
had finished and I was very touched ...

[Two days later] Joseph heard me return and has just given
me another card of St. Therese. I replied that I already had
one, thank you, but he wasn't taking no for an answer and
thrust it into my hand in any case, along with a calendar in
French from 'Les Missionnaires D'Afrique'. Every day the
calendar lists at least one saint's feast day – today's saint is
St Beatrice apparently. I wonder what she got up to. St
Edouard is the 5 January.

And then there was the beautiful Céleste, a first year PhD
student and the Foyer secretary and accountant, who was
'cute and modest and kind and by the fourth finger on her
left hand, certainly single'.

Céleste really is sensational, with the most adorable French
voice. I absolutely cursed myself when my French broke
down as I chatted to her, as [in] our previous encounter it
had been very good indeed. I often now imagine a life with
Céleste in a gorgeous Lebanese stone villa from the 1930s,
feeling satisfied and in love as we do our bit to restore the
jewel of the Middle East, simply by being free and talented
and wealthy. I really do need to calm down on this fantasy a
touch. I'm sure she isn't nearly as struck by me as I am by
her and I seem to have become something of a Lebanese
nostalgic hard-liner, despite having been here not even two
weeks and despite not knowing anything really about
Lebanese politics. In any case, how am I even going to
communicate effectively with Céleste, eh? Let alone sweep-

ing her off her feet and marrying her. I must have a plan for this!

Their conversation two days later proved no more satisfactory:

> My French totally and inexplicably and infuriatingly broke down again as I tried to explain to Céleste, looking as beautiful as ever, that I would like her to write an official document saying that I would be at the Foyer until the end of March, and that I would like her to tell me how to print off some emails in my inbox from USJ certifying that I am indeed studying there. Things aren't helped by the fact that invariably these days, my first contact with Céleste is over an internal phone from the porter's lodge type area – despite her actual office only being 10 yards away. I remain terrible at speaking French with people I cannot see – in fact my telephone manner in English is pretty bad as I tend to stammer. At one stage we have to humiliatingly move into English, something which was rather a struggle for Céleste actually. My subsequent fluency with my Austrian friend Mikhael and the far less attractive other office girl only serves to infuriate me further.

Eddie also made friends with some local residents, whom he met after mass at the Jounieh Catholic church. Matthieu, in particular, was to become a good friend, and Ed spent some time with his family:

> … by far the most important event of the day [9 February] was the dinner with Matthieu and his family, the people I had met on the steps after Church on Sunday. Having previously run out of money on the Foyer pay phone trying to call his mobile two days earlier, I called him up better prepared this time and arranged to meet outside the Foyer at 8pm. I had made the faux-pas of assuming that the attractive Senegalese woman he introduced me to after church, Marie-Thérèse, was his wife. I am sure that is what he said. Anyway, asking him to remind me of his Senegalese wife's name, he told me that he remained single. Oh dear! Anyway,

Matthieu turned out to live only about 3 minutes walk away
from the Foyer, in a beautiful old pre-war Lebanese house,
made from that typical dark-yellow stone. He said he had
lived there all his life. As we went through his garden gate, it
became instantly clear that Matthieu belonged to that old
Lebanese Christian upper class, the sort of family I had not
really yet met. In the porch-way, he introduced me to his
incredibly cute and well-behaved dog, Ito (I think) a big,
tame, fluffy thing which had lots of Alsatian in him. He
asked me to put some elasticated covers over my shoes as his
mother wouldn't want any mud brought in but the stone
floors within would make bare feet intolerable. We said hello
to the Sri Lankan maid-servants before greeting his parents.
His (French) mother [Françoise] was lying on the floor in the
dark on some oriental cushions, smoking and watching a
documentary about seventeenth century style old Germanic
puritans living in a religious colony in Belize, complete with
an old Germanic language and dress, a total dedication to
their very low-church Christianity. It took no time at all to
recognize Françoise as an aging hippy in her 50s. The whole
house was kitted out with mattresses on the floor under
patterned cloth awnings for their beds, well-made wooden
furniture, polished stone floors with rugs here and there and
large cushions on the floor for sofas. This beautiful old
house, its decoration, their manner and French language
marked this family out as well-established and prosperous.

I had my first alcohol of my stay before supper, a fantastic fortified walnut wine made by the mother herself; I take
it from ingredients grown in their own garden. Over a deli-
cious dinner, a mix of traditional Sri Lankan and Lebanese
[food], they were an absolute delight to be with. I sat next to
Françoise who was excellent fun, totally forthright, leaning
forward towards me to make her opinions emphatically. She
was quick and very keen to correct my French, for which I
was most grateful. The subjects we talked about were very
academic and wide ranging – the British Empire featured
greatly after I joked that I was always pleased to see Sri
Lankans because they were the only ones in the country who
could understand cricket. Jaques [Matthieu's father]
mentioned that he had only ever been thrown out of an
establishment once in his life for not wearing a tie, and that

was in Colombo – 'they can be more British than the British'. We discussed why we hadn't thrown Abu Hamza al-Masri into prison earlier and from there got onto the Polish flying with the RAF in World War II, the Huguenots fleeing to England, La Reine Margot, Bloody Mary of England and the Jews of the Middle Ages. All the time, Françoise would firmly but politely correct my French when needed – I could do with that every day. She said that after one month with their family, I would be fluent. I really wish I could take them up on that.

Jaques had lived in Cambridge with his Swiss girl friend in the 1950s and relayed many happy stories from his time [there] – although of all of them he seemed the least inclined to speak to me in French. He is the absolute paradigm of the type of free-thinking, free-living, well-educated and nostalgic Christian which powered the Lebanon to the very heights of its pre-war civil, artistic and economic glory. Perhaps the Christians did it [to] share the wealth, power and prestige of the nation with their Muslim compatriots. I don't know and what is certain is that the war was certainly not so simple as a civil conflict between Lebanese Muslims and Christians, but rather Lebanon acted as a location where neighbouring nations and tribes played out their murderous differences. But I look around at the tower block scarred hillsides of today, the mountains of national debt, the Hezbollah fundamentalists sitting in government and I see that it's a long way back for this country to its glorious reputation of yester year. Perhaps it is simply impossible, in any case, for other countries in the region to allow a totally free and wealthy Lebanon to happily exist in itself – as its freedoms and liberty would no doubt cause instability in their oppressed and dirt poor populations looking enviously on. Perhaps this country will always be interfered with and picked at by others so that it can never recover its past.

A few days later, Ed was again invited to Matthieu's home:

After the service I went for a walk with Matthieu and Marie-Thérèse, the Senegalese woman who I mistakenly thought was his wife last week. He kindly walked me to the local security bureau, where I could apply for a visa extension the

next day. As we walked, Marie-Thérèse mentioned that she
would like to learn English and I offered my services. Fixing
up a time in the week proved tricky. I wrote down my email
address but it didn't sound as though she had regular email
access. I couldn't give her a phone number, of course. And
she didn't seem keen to have Matthieu and I over for dinner
during the week. I'm not sure how this will progress, therefore.

Matthieu kindly invited me over for Sunday lunch back at
his [place] and I gladly accepted. He introduced me to a
family which lodges in the outhouse in his wild, spacious
garden. They too were incredibly talented interior-designers
and arty-types – long-haired, neckerchiefs, chunky clothes
that looked home-knitted. Their place was beautifully set-
up, as you'd expect, and also as you'd expect from
terrifically educated, well-to-do bohemians the louche décor
of the house and its inhabitants was accompanied by deluxe
electrical gadgetry: super lap-tops and heaters and sound
systems and long low sofas and hippy floor cushions. I was
introduced to their 5 year old daughter, Saloue, who was
very, very cute, but perhaps a little spoilt. It looked as
though she could do with a little brother or sister . . .

Lunch was taken upstairs in the old house. This floor was
for the grandparents and had become a little run-down since
their deaths. But what rooms! Enormous windows letting in
the natural light, hugely tall ceilings creating a wonderful
atmosphere of space, and a huge veranda with gorgeous
white pillars. After lunch Jaques took me out there to show
me the fruit trees in the garden. Once upon a time all of
Jounieh looked like this. As we looked towards the sea
Jaques pointed out where Syrian shells had landed during the
war. They were trying to destroy the harbour but many shells
fell short. Over lunch, another beautiful affair prepared by
the Sri Lankan maids full of fresh, healthy Mediterranean
cheeses and bread and dips, the conversation moved to
Lebanese Politics, and I asked questions about the leading
figures around today. Who is Waled Jumblatt and what is he
like? – that sort of thing. It turned out that Emile Lahoude
was a family friend and that the father and he had often gone
diving together. For the second time, I was told that unfor-
tunately Lahoude was like a snake, far too willing to play the

Syrian game. Apparently the Syrians have gerrymandered the Lebanese electoral map and constituency boundaries so that the Christian population – which is spread evenly throughout the country – everywhere finds itself in the minority in the various constituencies.

The chat was fascinating but I was sorry that I had kept it going so long. Matthieu by the end really was looking very distressed. He explained to me that he simply couldn't bear to consider Lebanese politics any more. It was too dirty, too complicated and too oppressive. Now, after years and years he could only bear to think about himself, the welfare of his family and friends. He told me that he was a pessimist, the glass always half-full – he simply didn't want to consider the political world. I felt terribly sorry for him. He's in his mid-late 30s: he grew up and went to school with bombs landing all around him. He saw the beautiful old Jounieh of his childhood literally blown up around him. Now it has been replaced by ugly tower blocks, '*une désastre fantastique*', and by a more materialistic money-obsessed people. For a gentle, beauty-loving, bohemian architect, this situation is very difficult to take indeed. The sense of nostalgia almost moved me to tears. As I left after lunch, I said goodbye to Matthieu in his bedroom and found him smoking a spliff. Despite the hippy décor and attitude all around me, this still took me a little by surprise. He said that he was stressed out by the amount of work he had on. I wondered whether I had brought back too many unhappy memories for him and felt awful and tactless.

In his final diary entry, Eddie revealed that he planned to make and send a thank-you card to Matthieu and his family on the theme of Catullus, poem 13. We do not know whether he did this, but we were able to meet and thank a shaken Matthieu in person shortly after Eddie's death. Matthieu's Jounieh number is still on my mobile that I had loaned to Ed before his departure.

It is clear that Eddie was getting the most out of his cultural experiences in Lebanon. The church services he attended made a distinct impression – and, not least, in terms of the dedication of the Lebanese Christians to their cultural identity – as is revealed by these diary extracts (for 7 and 12 February) describing a Syriac Catholic mid-week morning mass and an Armenian Catholic Sunday service:

Now, I am not too sure of the doctrinal nuances involved with Syriac Catholicism but since 8.30am I can tell you something about their services. The priest is dressed in a very glitzy outfit. There is plenty of ancient sounding chanting, often led by two male members of the congregation standing at the front of the Church. I suppose they would be like our precentors. The responses from the rest of the congregation were always vigorous, none of the half-hearted mumblings too often found back home.

The chapel itself was quite dark with plenty of the types of icons and candles found in Joseph's room. There was a large portrait of (I presume) St Antoine, dressed in black, behind the altar which completely dwarfed in size the crucifix on the altar itself. Joseph introduced me to Père Antoine, the priest, and after we had exchanged '*enchantés*' I was sat down at the front on the right hand side. I would have preferred to observe from the back really. Right in front of me there was a huge statue of the Madonna with a rosary draped around her. This was balanced by a similar-sized statue of Christ on the left hand side of the chapel. Joseph rather optimistically gave me a service book in Syriac to follow. Père Antoine was a man, I guessed, in his late 30s with a rather bulbous nose and lightly slicked-back hair. On occasions, he would give a little yawn during the service, which I thought was a bit off – but it certainly was a well attended chapel. This was a weekday 8am mass, in a small side chapel in part of what is (at best) only the third most popular Christian church in Lebanon, which is a minority Christian nation in any case. I would say about 60 people were there for all, or part of the time. Really very healthy indeed. I couldn't help but notice that as the priest read out the gospel, one of the icon candles held either side of the precentors still had its price tag on it ...

Following the service this Sunday was rather easier than last time as I found the order of service in the front of the little blue books. The singing in church really is pleasingly enthusiastic. Needless to say, the hymns we sing aren't a patch on Hymns Ancient and Modern or the Methodist

Hymn Book or other such things in our wonderful English tradition, but the French songs we do get through are heartily bashed out nonetheless. They are accompanied by a girl (c.17 years) on an electric clavinova thing. The sound it makes is rather in the manner of 'pigeon in flight' and '500 Bus Stops' tune, which makes me smile but it's not the most important thing I suppose. The acoustics in the white-washed church are appalling and I find following the sermon a little tricky because of this, sadly. It is worth noting, again, that attendance is very good. The pews are very busy indeed, especially remarkable since the 10.30 is only one of three morning masses on Sundays.

The prayer service in the Romanesque crusader church of St Marc and St Jean at Jbail-Byblos – which reminded Eddie of the Temple church – was rather different, consisting 'only of about six active participants who would take in turns to stand up and chant prayers in a repetitive manner. I think I heard a lot of prayers for peace (*Salaam*) upon various people and also chants of 'blessed are the such and such (*Murabate)'*. Still on the hottest and clearest day of his early stay, Eddie had a wonderful time wandering around the famous crusader complex, and was even inspired to send a post-card to his former History teacher who had nurtured his love for the period.

Eddie was also spending his time catching up on his reading and working on classical translations. He enjoyed *A Farewell to Arms*, although, having finished it, he sighed: 'Where will my Catherine Barkley come from?' Oscar Wilde was much less favourably judged than Hemingway, and his short stories gained a decidedly poor review. Ed became bored in *The Portrait of Mr W. H.* with 'Wilde's shameless and ... tedious display of learning'; he 'wasn't hugely wowed' by *The Young King*; and he found *The Fisherman and his Soul* to be:

the most fantastical bullshit of the very worst romanticised nineteenth century kind, from first word to last. A mark of shame in the Wilde canon in fact. It's dedicated to Alice,

Princess of Monaco, and I hope she was furious. It's
less than 34 pages long in my edition and at various
stages I was literally groaning out loud with tedium and
embarrassment.

Eddie had brought some works by Propertius, Catullus,
Aristophanes and Sophocles with him to Lebanon, and
found these texts much more to his taste, although on
4 February he wrote:

> I was also furious with myself for being so poor at translat-
> ing Catullus a day or two ago – after so many years I really
> do feel I should be much better than I am. But turning *The
> Commodores* into Latin for some of the OH [Old Herefor-
> dian] classics crowd (*semel, bis ter, Venustam et te amo etc*)
> was enjoyable and seems to have gone down well. They had
> actually asked me to translate Aristophanes' *Clouds* into
> English, and so really they got something totally different to
> what they were asking for and something utterly useless too.
> *The Clouds* work best start tomorrow.

Over the following weeks, Ed worked hard at 'creating my
own translation' of *The Clouds* for 'Kaloi k'Agathoi', Hereford Cathedral School's classical drama company. In the
weeks before he left England, the company had been
formally constituted with the aim of putting on a classical
drama each year 'to promote interest in classical theatre
among young people in the March and beyond'. It was one
of Eddie's tasks while he was away to translate Aristophanes' comedy for performance at the Three Choirs'
Festival 'fringe' in August 2006. He set about the project
with relish and was generally pleased with his efforts. As he
confided to his diary on 11 February:

> I was also very pleased to make good progress with my next
> chunk of Aristophanes – the jokes and lines really are
> flowing at the moment, and also a good manipulation of and
> adherence to the original Greek: I'm not just [going] my own
> way with only passing reference to the actual text. However,
> my best lines so far are mostly regarding a violent anal sex

and aggressive bestial rape, which is a touch worrying – if in keeping with the spirit of the original.

Eddie was clearly exaggerating for effect here. As his Classics teacher later explained '*Clouds* is a satire on academia and philosophy and there is hardly any sex and certainly no rape, violence or bestiality. The worst he could come up with was a lot of foul language which was causing much controversy back home'. In his final email to his 'luvvy' friends of 4 April, written hours before he died, it is good (although heart-breaking) to read that 'as the loyal son of a former HM', he was prepared to tone down the racier bits of his script to save his old school from potential embarrassment. Ed had repeatedly asked for their thoughts. 'What do you think about this plan? ... Please let me know ... And don't be at all shy. As I've told Al, I'm not precious about this process in any way'. As it transpired, although some of the political jokes were cut, Eddie would have been pleased to have known, after all his hard work, that in the eventual production of *The Clouds* (first performed in 2007) most of his adaptation (Ed later admitted to 'token connections' between some of his song lyrics and the original Greek) of Aristophanes' original play survived intact.

But life for Eddie in Lebanon was not all plain sailing. Aside from the difficulty of translating Aristophanes for his friends from a distance of thousands of miles and in something of a vacuum – 'What I need is for people to confirm that they like these ideas', he mildly complained, '... It is great fun putting all this together but it will also be a massive waste of time, if the stuff is more or less entirely binned by the directors come this summer' – there were also the frustrations which inevitably accompanied a foreigner living in a strange country.

His anxieties had little to do with the fragile political situation. A diary entry reveals that he witnessed the 5 February riot in Beirut but only on television:

I've only been here since Tuesday, and I witnessed my first
serious riot. Hezbollah had organised some violence in
Beirut outside the Danish Embassy. They clashed with a
small group of Christians who were there demonstrating to
support the Danish government's refusal to censor their own
press and to support the idea of free expression more generally. On TV tonight, I saw how badly beaten some of the
Christians were by the Hezbollah thugs. Hezbollah trashed
the Danish Embassy, smashed up vehicles, stoned the police
and fire brigade and generally caused mayhem. There were
literally 1,000s of them. Even their well meaning clerics
couldn't hold them back. The idea of blaming 'a few bad
apples' simple won't wash. This was highly organised, highly
politicised, well attended Islamic violence.

Nine days later, however, on 14 February, the anniversary of
the Hariri assassination, having bought a Lebanese flag, he
was present at a demonstration in Beirut, protesting against
Syrian interference in Lebanon 'and waved around the
Lebanese flag for a while and wandered around the
crowded centre ville'. This was not quite in keeping with his
mother's email request that he should 'keep a nice low
profile . . . [and] steer well clear of demos or the like', but he
obviously felt that he would not be noticed in a crowd of a
million. A little later (in emails marked 'not dead') he joked
to a friend: 'I am yet to be captured by Hezbollah or
Hamas. In fact if you ignore the trashing of various
embassies it really doesn't seem too dangerous at all'. More
reassuringly, he later wrote:

> . . . don't fret about my safety too much. It's very tough out
> here if you are a public figure trying to rid the country of
> malign external influence, but otherwise people are delight-
> ful! And I have already learned to say in good Arabic, 'no
> I'm British not American', which always cheers people up.
> There is no street crime of any sort out here (lucky, really, as
> there is no civilian police force either . . .) and I am probably
> safer here at night than female students are walking across
> Magd bridge.

Eddie was much more concerned about the trials of daily living than his own safety. As we have seen, he was hard on himself when his French collapsed at the crucial moment, especially when chatting up beautiful girls. He was also annoyed when the electricity supply cut out as it did several times each day and the computer or phone connections were severed. And he invariably got lost during his early trips into Beirut, and was exasperated by Lebanese bureaucracy when he tried to extend his visa, as shown by these diary entries for 8 and 13 February:

Having failed to get access to Céleste to chat about directions to the British Embassy in Beirut, I simply called them up. A man with a thick accent at the other end couldn't have been less helpful. I'm quickly learning that although people here say 'just ask someone if you get lost anywhere', the Lebanese are totally and utterly helpless with directions. Mainly because there are no ... street names or building numbers. Madness ...

Needless to say, I was, a few hours later, hopelessly lost in central Beirut in an extended and spectacular downpour, the water pouring through the holes in my shoes. I did get to see the spectacular new mosque, some nice churches and the very smartly rebuilt 'down town' area, the shops and flats do look very plush indeed. But I was absolutely amazed that my French was now getting me nowhere at all. My louder and louder and more desperate pleas of *'pour aller à l'Ambassade Britannique'* were simply met with, at best 'no English, no English'. Perhaps it's a Muslim thing to have no French. Anyway, I jumped into a cab, who also had no idea where to go, who then asked his friend. He drove me approximately 90 seconds to the right place and demanded $5,000. I argued with him for a while but then just handed it over.

The security at the Embassy was very tight indeed and the building itself seemed gloomy and uninviting – it possibly is but my mood didn't help. In any case, I had been utterly soaked and ripped off for no reason at all. The lady on the internal phone (she WOULDN'T come even down some stairs to see me) said she could be of no help at all. I needed to go to a central Lebanese authority who were now closed for the day – and would be closed all Thursday, Friday, Saturday and Sunday too. She refused to even give directions, as it would be too complicated and difficult – surprise, surprise. Ludicrously, the best that can be done is to get a Lebanese friend call her on Monday morning – two days before my visa expires – to explain it to them and have the Lebanese friend accompany me from Jounieh to there. INCREDIBLY annoying. I did at least take the opportunity to collar the Embassy personnel manager in a different area of the building. She was bright and chirpy enough and gave me her email address, onto which I could plonk a message and cv. She did admit they were short staffed but didn't know what the situation would be re part-time or voluntary work.

I staggered back through the traffic to Jounieh, to catch up on some sleep. I get up again at mid-day to try and find Céleste to organise some paper-work before extending my visa at the local security office in Jounieh. I get together my passport, a statement from Banque Audi acknowledging my first transfer from England and my receipt for Feb's rent at the Foyer ... At about 1.40pm, Père Toni brought through the documents into the computer room where I was chatting confidently and fluently in French with my Austrian friend, Mikhael. I went over to the local bureau straight away only to be told, without explanation, to come back tomorrow. They simply couldn't be bothered. I was warned to expect an unhelpful attitude from both Mikhael and Matthieu but I really wasn't in the mood to take it. It certainly reminded me of Sam Mallett's non-PC warning back in Hereford that if you ask an Arab to do something for you, the first reply will invariably be '*Bokra*'. So I'll have to knock on their doors again at 8am and condemn myself to being hours late for my first class at USJ which may well be of the wrong standard in any case.

And then there were the further difficulties which he experienced on 10 and 13 February concerning the inefficiencies of Lebanon's public transport and the chaotic administration of his university department:

This time I made it to USJ without getting lost at all, the

second bus understanding my request for the Mathaf, Ashrafieh without problems and getting through the ridiculously jammed streets reasonably well. From the Mathaf I could recognize the human sciences building of USJ and was there after 2 or 3 minutes on foot. Of my class, I was the only one to turn up to this meeting which had been arranged to organize our time-table – perhaps the others were all more new to Beirut than I, and had got lost trying to find their way around, as seems obligatory. Despite filling out my form and applying for the 'faux debutant' classes I seem to have been put in the absolute beginner group. Having spent £100s in Hereford I really don't want to be wasting my time so I think I'll try the faux debutant classes at first and see if I can cope. 8.30 start on Monday – ugg. I was pleased to fight off my kind teacher's efforts to talk in English and we stuck to French; it went well. I'm clearly improving my navigation as I walked from USJ to centre ville without problems, and I am now writing from the pavement area of a plush boulangerie in the newly rebuilt area ...

Struggling out of bed, then, and moving very slowly I made it onto a bus by about 8.10am, hoping that 50 minutes would be enough for the journey. Beiruti pollution-filled traffic jams and miserable rain really combine horribly badly, especially when one of your fellow passengers starts smoking. I eventually made it through the traffic and got to the 5th floor of the USJ human sciences by 9.30, half an hour late. What's more an advanced Arabic class seemed to be going on in my room 507. I then looked more closely at the notice on the board, to see that my first session was due to start 'mardi', tomorrow. I couldn't believe it – yet another entirely wasted journey into Beirut in the pouring rain. I lost count time of the number of times I had said 'à lundi' to my teacher, when we organized the time-table on Friday. In fact I was the only one from our class to make it to that wretched meeting, and the times got changed arbitrarily in any case and no-one bothered to let me know. Infuriating.

As it happened, Eddie's worst fears were not realised. His class at the University Saint Joseph turned out to have suited him well, and with his early difficulties behind him, the final diary entry for 16 February ends on a characteristically positive note:

> At last, progress at USJ! After a good night's sleep, I was on the bus heading to Dowra at 7.50am and made good progress into town ... I was surprised to get myself onto a smart new bus, which Ken Livingstone would be glad to have on the streets of London. It made a pleasant change from the cramped, fume belching, barely road worthy little mini buses I usually take, which stop as often as they can in the search for more customers. The driver didn't have any change for my 10,000 LL note; I think he was just going to keep the lot until a friendly man in front sorted out the problem for me. I ended by handing over 1,200 in coins – double the normal price – obviously one has to pay for the express service and the clean environs. I got chatting in French with my friendly fellow passenger who had saved me all that money. He was called Pierre and was delighted to hear that I was staying at the foyer des Apôtres in Jounieh. The current Maronite general secretary, Fr Khalil Ahmed, who welcomed me on the first day in the Foyer, and who had been contacted from Oxford by Fr Shafiq Abouzayd on my behalf, had conducted his marriage service. A small world indeed.
>
> On time for the lesson at USJ and it was an absolute delight! The class consisted of three entirely French people, a girl born in Lebanon to Lebanese parents but who had lived in Nice from the age of two, an American from AUB. who is perfectly happy to chat in French, and myself. Just the kind of Franco-phone environment I'm looking for. The one other chap in the class is a solid fellow from Toulouse, so we got chatting about rugby. He's called Erwin, is here studying Phoenician and the history of religion at USJ, and Guilgamesh is his hotmail address. All pretty impressive, but I find his Toulouse accent a little difficult to follow. The two French girls are smart-looking students from Paris. I sat myself down next to Roula, the stunning-looking Franco-Libanaise. She was a law student back in France and would like to live over here and work as a company solicitor. She seems very proud of her middle Eastern roots, in a typically 2nd generation immigrant sort of way, and looked a little

put-out to be described as 'French' when in our class we practised each other's nationalities. Anyway, just being around her and the French girls, chatting in French and making friends, thoroughly cheered me up.

The class itself was conducted almost entirely in Arabic by our teacher Nada – a thoroughly cute and pleasant post graduate Lebanese student in her late twenties. Nada asked us all to assume Arab names for the purposes of the class. Poor Erwin, when asked which name he would like, rather feeling the pressure blurted out the first Arab name which came into his head. Osama. A touch embarrassing. After umming and arring, I eventually plumped for Azar, thinking about the chap who talked to me on the street in Jounieh and also the Pakistani cricketer, Azar Mahmood. I did, though, rather regret this choice, as I would have naturally preferred to go for a name which an Arab Christian would be happy with, such as Ibrahim, Yousuf, or Emile. Not many Christians [are] called Azar, I reckon. After the successful class, I took down everyone's email address and promised to be in touch. The last one I said goodbye to was Erwin who really liked the idea of meeting up to watch some six nations at the

A Beirut Arabic class, University Saint Joseph, *c* February 2006

weekend and perhaps going out as well. Looks like I could
become good friends with this lot.

I was clearly on a lucky streak and as even my bus journey
home was a great success: one bus direct from the Mathaf to
my Jounieh bridge and little traffic on the road. I was even
picked up by the very mini-bus driver who had dropped me
off two days earlier, and had kindly returned a 10,000 LL
note I had accidentally given him wrapped up inside the
other one ... for my new shoes. [His old ones were badly
worn and had leaked.]

That afternoon, Ed emailed his brother, following his
nephew's birth a few days earlier, to say he was 'feeling very
chirpy after the morning's success'.

Eddie presumably did not have sufficient time to keep a
diary once his Arabic classes (nine hours of tuition, spread
over four days a week) had started. His final weeks in
Lebanon, therefore, are less well documented. Nevertheless, despite the occasional rant – we received one furious
email on 25 March from an enraged Ed after Orange had
continued to charge him £15 per month for his mobile
after he had cancelled the contract – there is every reason
to believe that he was enjoying life. He did indeed make
good friends with the students in his Arabic class, all of
whom were French speaking which pleased him – a
'friendly Francophone bunch', he called them – although
in politics they were much too Europeanist for his liking.
As previously, his French kept breaking down when he got
too excited. As he told Nicholas Purcell, his former Oxford
tutor, on 6 March:

> The language is very well appreciated around town among
> the Jounieh Christians, but when I try and say things rather
> more involved than shopping requests to my French friends
> at the university, I fall flat on my face. I could only splutter
> impotently when one of them said that there should be a
> single European head of state governing the whole continent
> and that, no, there was no significant financial mismanage-
> ment at the heart of the European Commission. Mon Dieu!

His Arabic was going well. One of his friends later confided that he was the best in the class, despite his difficulty in rolling his rs which impeded his pronunciation, and his teachers considered him to have been an exemplary student who was 'always smiling'. Again, however, he was not entirely satisfied with his progress, or at least with simply learning formal written Arabic. 'I don't want to go around talking like a newspaper, so I am currently on the hunt for a tutor in colloquial Arabic', he wrote in the same letter to his tutor. But it was his lack of fluency in French that was his chief concern.

Indeed, Ed's lack of opportunity for speaking French with fellow students in his hall of residence was one of the main causes of dissatisfaction with his Jounieh accommodation. As early as 8 February he had written in his diary that his failure to socialise with people of his own age was 'a real disappointment'. And (as he told us later that month) there was also the problem of the 11pm curfew, and 'at weekends I have to wait for Père Toni to return for him to function the internet service etc etc ... but most of all I am worried about the language sitch'. Before the end of February he had made it clear that he was hoping to move in with Matthieu's family for a while but was it ethical, Eddie asked, to move so soon when he had committed himself to staying at the Foyer until the end of March? Unless he could be released from his undertaking, the right answer was obviously no – he should honour his agreement. The move to Matthieu's family home did not prove possible so Ed was spared that particular ethical dilemma.

Eddie then started looking for an apartment near the university, but it was not until he had found accommodation at the Hotel St Joseph, Jounieh, for our visit in April that he thought about staying there himself:

You will simply LOVE the hotel I have told you about [he emailed on 17 March]. The lady who runs it is charming, it is situated in the most attractive part of town with beautiful old-style Lebanese architecture all round, you'll get a sea view, a huge terrace to lounge around on etc etc. All in all, go for it! It's slightly run down, but it is full of character and charm – not rats! ... She's even offered to put me up for $120 for April, if all else fails. We had a lovely chat in French for 30 mins or so, much more French than I usually get!

The following day Heather replied: 'Dad certainly thought that her offer of $120 for April was well worth considering'. It is to my eternal regret that I ever made that remark.

One week later, having discovered a flat near the university that he liked, Ed was still trying to find a 'franco-phone flat-mate' to share it with. 'Please pile in the prayers that some-one turns up', he wrote. Heather replied: 'Will pile in the prayers for your accommodation situation. Dad and I do pray for you on a daily basis! Will re-double efforts – perhaps God's busy (joke!) or has other plans?'

Eddie moved to his small room in the Hotel St Joseph, in the rain, on the week-end of 1st and 2nd April, following the party to celebrate Diane (a fellow student's) birthday when he danced the night away. It was quite an exhausting move, he informed us in his final email on 3 April, 'but all will settle down soon!' That afternoon, he phoned to wish me a happy birthday. It was the last time we heard his voice. Heather then sent him an air mail letter, together with a post-card showing a boating crew 'in view of Oxford's success against the light blues in the boat race'. Both arrived posthumously. A few days earlier, Eddie had emailed a friend:

Really, despite the drama of recent messages, I'm perfectly happy at the moment and it's not as if I have suddenly become a total wreck or anything. As ever, I'll just keep life ticking over and I have no doubt it will continue to surprise and delight.

Chapter 4

Our Via Dolorosa

After some initial doubts as to whether we should go to visit Eddie in the Lebanon, Heather and I arrived at Beirut airport on the evening of Thursday 6 April, a week before Maundy Thursday. The place was full of visitors like us but mainly of families returning to the Lebanon for the Easter holidays – which meant that Heather and I had been unable to sit next to each other on the plane, more than inconvenience given Heather's distaste for flying. But the flight itself was uneventful. I had spent most of the time untroubled, reading Fr Donovan's, *Christianity Rediscovered* – 'one of those rare books', according to the *Methodist Recorder,* 'which changes the way you look at the world' – in preparation for an ordination selection panel which was less than four months away. My reading was interspersed with interesting conversations with the young man sitting next to me. He was a Lebanese-born architect who had been working in London – he had recently bought his first flat in Clapham, I recall – and who was returning to his family in Beirut for Easter. Towards the end of the journey, he carefully selected a cut-glass broach from the in-flight catalogue as a present for his girl friend. The young architect assured me that Jounieh, where Ed had taken up residence and where the architect's family lived, was a most beautiful suburb and that we would have a wonderful time in the Lebanon. We disembarked into a sultry Lebanese evening with great anticipation at the prospect both of visiting the Middle East for the first time and, above all, of seeing Eddie again more than nine weeks after leaving him at Heathrow.

In retrospect, the first sign of anything amiss at Beirut Airport was being met by the airport manager, shepherded into his office and 'fast-tracked' through Customs. Our holiday visa, too, after an initial delay, was personally delivered. Not that at the time we were any way worried by these turn of events. Eddie, before his departure, had already made contact with Ian, the Old Herefordian working in Beirut, who had been immensely supportive of Eddie in his first few days in the Lebanon. We assumed that Ian, as an Embassy Warden, was simply extending a helping hand through Customs to the former Headmaster of his old school. While we were waiting for the visa, I remember Heather characteristically helping an exhausted young mother by occupying her child for a few moments. That Eddie could not be seen at the barrier to meet us was not an undue cause for alarm – he was invariably late and we knew from his communications that Beirut traffic could be horrendous. It was only when we had finally crossed that barrier and were ushered into what seemed like a broom-cupboard to meet Chris Poole and Trudy Curry, the Deputy Ambassador and Vice-Consul at the British Embassy, that our world was shattered by their dreadful news. At first, we did not hear beyond the words 'we have been informed by the police ...' Why was Eddie of all people in trouble with the police? It took some moments before we realised that we were being told that he had in fact died.

The next 36 hours was a time of frenetic activity, blurred vision, numbness and unknown sorrow. We were whisked back from the airport to the British Embassy in a black limousine, trying to make polite conversation in the knowledge that a parent's worse night-mare had in our case come true. At the Embassy, our first need was to make contact with our three other children. This proved impossible in the case of Clare, who was on holiday in Spain with her own family, but too soon we were relaying our appalling news over the Vice-Consul's mobile to Michael in Dorset and then to Sarah in London. Meanwhile, Stella Major, the Embassy Doctor, had been ascertaining whether we could see Eddie's body, which had been moved to Baabda Hospital, immediately. That proved to be impossible to arrange until the following morning, and so we were taken, via a drug-store, to a nearby hotel to try to gather ourselves for the following day's ordeal. Despite the comfort of the Beirut hotel, which was far more luxurious than Eddie's Jounieh hostel where we had intended to stay, sleep was intermittent at best, and our stumbling prayers – we recited the Evening Office together – proved more efficacious than the sleeping-draft. Heather later confided that the chorus, 'I will raise him up', kept ringing around her brain that night and helped maintain her sanity, if not induce sleep.

We were met outside the hotel at 11 the next morning by the Embassy driver, who was to negotiate the teeming Beirut traffic with such skill throughout the day, together with Stella Major and Trudy Curry. On the way to the hospital, we picked up the coroner who had examined Eddie when he was discovered at the hostel the previous day. And then, when we arrived at the hospital morgue – which looked to us more like a bomb-shelter – there was an unconscionable delay before we could view Ed's body. Eventually, we obtained the necessary permissions to see our beloved son, his body covered in a dirty green sheet, his head wrapped in his by now bloody towel, the dark blood stains merging with the image of the red Welsh dragon with which it was embroidered. Although hard to identify, there was no doubt that this bloated corpse was Eddie's earthly remains – his 50 stitch scar, resulting from the fall through a skylight on the roof of the Oxford Union, being clearly visible on his left leg. Heather touched his foot and said a quick prayer over the body before we were pushed out of the dark chamber, rather too smartly, into the streaming light of Beirut's midday sun.

From the hospital, we were driven across Beirut again towards the Jounieh hostel where Eddie had spent his last few days. The traffic was all that Ed had described it to be

some five weeks earlier on the back of a picture post-card
(or 'postie' as he liked to call them) of the Rue Weygand: 'I
simply can't think when this photo would have been taken.
Where are all the taxis reversing against the traffic flow?
Where the fully-leaded clouds of pollution? Where the
pedestrians blindly crossing whenever they feel liked it? All
far too organised ...' As if to emphasise the point, our
excellent driver abandoned the car at a road junction to buy
us a snack lunch at the best falafel take-away in town. It
was gratefully received – our churning stomachs had taken
in little over the previous 24 hours. Once on the highway
our progress was uninterrupted until we reached the
Jounieh hostel, where the police had been patiently waiting
several hours for our arrival.

The Hotel St Joseph was a former Mayor's residence in
the centre of Jounieh. The 'Lonely Planet' guide, which I
had bought Ed just before he left, considered it to be 'a
shabby but character-filled pension run by a charming
English woman', a view enthusiastically endorsed by Eddie
just a few days before, prior to his move there the previous
week-end. This was confirmed by our own observations.
The Mediterranean could be glimpsed from the huge roof
terrace and the place was surrounded by old-style Lebanese
buildings of the French colonial period. Not that we had the
slightest inclination to view the sea or admire the surrounding architecture, despite having to wait several hours for the
police to complete the formalities – three lengthy documents
in Arabic which all had to be counter-signed before we
could collect Eddie's effects. Meanwhile, we learned from
Maria, the aforesaid charming manageress, who had
discovered Eddie the previous morning and was the last
person to have seen him alive, that he had been cheerfully
cooking a meal late on that Tuesday evening, talking excit-
edly about our visit. 'You must tell my mother that I can
cook!' he had said, as he prepared his late night and last
supper. He had apparently gone to bed happy and full of
anticipation – that, at least, was a small crumb of comfort.

His cramped bedsit was just as he had left it that last

Tuesday night, messy but ordered, his desk covered by his open Greek lexicon and text of Aristophanes' *Clouds*, which he was translating for Kaloi k'Agathoi, the school's classical theatre company, his note-paper, some Arabic exercises and a French dictionary. It was as though he had just popped out to the shops for five minutes and would soon be returning. The documents signed, we collected his things together in the suitcase he had bought from Chadd's department store in Hereford those few weeks before. Before departing, the police-chief showed us some images from his digital camera of Eddie's body, slumped as it had been found on the bed, slightly bloody but more recognisably Eddie than the darkened corpse we had seen that morning. He had also discovered on Ed's mobile the phone number of Matthieu, Ed's Jounieh friend from the Catholic church, who hurried down to see us before our departure. Matthieu was distraught with grief and promised to have a Mass said for his dead friend the following Sunday. Having thanked him, we explained that we would not now be staying in Jounieh, said our good-byes and took our leave.

Once we knew that it would not be possible for Edward's body to be repatriated for several days at least, we decided to return to England the following day, less than 48 hours after our arrival. Leaving him in Lebanon was hard but there seemed no point in remaining in the country now that Eddie had died. This gave Trudy less than an hour to change our airline tickets, which she successfully accomplished on her return to the Embassy. Meanwhile, we accepted an invitation from the Deputy Ambassador, Chris Poole and his wife, Lynne, to unwind at their beautiful flat over-looking Beirut. It was a very kind gesture which was gratefully received. The most pleasant part of that punishing day was their hospitality and our conversation, extraordinarily enough, about Herefordshire where they planned to live on their retirement. As touching in its way was the Lebanese driver's condolences, in halting English, as we returned to our hotel. 'I know how you feel', he said, 'because I too have lost a child'.

Beirut

We were high in the air and over sea winging,
Although I hate flying, my heart was singing.
We were off to Beirut to visit our son –
I just couldn't wait 'til the journey was done!

We landed and then we were ushered straight through.
'The Embassy's sending an envoy for you.'
I protested and said, 'Our son should be here.'
The airport official appeared not to hear.

We waited nearby for the envoy to come,
And meanwhile I helped a very tired Mum
By playing and laughing with her little child,
Who, fed up with waiting, was about to run wild.

At last they arrived and guided us in
To a room not much bigger than a large biscuit tin.
'We're waiting,' I told them, 'For our son Ed.'
Then came the response, 'I'm afraid your son's dead.'

With heart wrenched in two I gave a great scream -
'This cannot be true! Please say it's a dream!
Oh No! No!' I cried, 'Oh, No! Dear God, No!
Please tell me, I beg you, that it isn't so!'

'Oh Eddie, my darling, why didn't you stay
Until we arrived, and then slip away
Quietly cradled, my holding your hand,
Not dying alone in this foreign land!'

I leapt up and scrabbled and scratched at the wall.
Hysteria rising, I scratched at the wall.
Then Howard rushed round to be at my side,
We clung to each other, we cried and we cried.

Some minutes later we went in a car
To the Embassy building – it wasn't too far.
Through all the security, led by our guide,
It took quite a while to get us inside.

They gave us some tea; they gave us a phone,
They gave us some space, and then we rang home.
At the news all the children were shocked to the core.
'Mum, what has happened? Are you quite sure?'

The phone calls once over the doctor arrived
To check that our health the bad news had survived.
I wanted that instant to look at our son,
But she assured me it couldn't be done.

What a sad night! Both sad and unreal,
Our poor shattered hearts did not know what to feel.
We clung to each other all through the night,
Now sobbing, now sighing, just holding on tight.

Next day we were taken to see our dear Ed.
In shocking conditions they'd kept our son, Ed.
We were not to touch him, just look at him, dead,
And confirm to the doctor 'It is our son, Ed.'

Falafel were bought us to help lift the gloom,
Then off we were driven to visit Ed's room.
The traffic was dreadful, the driver was great!
Much dodging and swerving – yet still we were late.

Familiar clothes were hanging on hooks,
Laid on his desk were his pen and his books.
It seemed he had just popped out for a while
And soon would return with his usual broad smile.

Three policemen wrote slowly, and one at a time
Reports and disclaimers they asked H to sign.
We then were allowed to take home Ed's stuff.
H signed them. We left. We'd had quite enough!

Chris had invited us back to his flat
Where we sat and relaxed and had a good chat.
We had much in common, it helped ease the pain.
Then back to our room we went once again.

We wanted to leave the very next day
For indeed we had now no more reason to stay.
Trudy worked fast – Yes! Our tickets would do
And Ed's luggage was cleared, it all could go through.

We wept as we flew on the first morning flight,
Our hearts were like lead, in our eyes shone no light.
How different life seemed from when we had left –
Then high excitement, now just bereft.

Once more with our children we hugged and we cried,
They all were distraught that our Eddie had died.
We talked to them too of kindnesses shown
By people we'd met there, but not before known.

It will take us a life-time to understand why
Someone as lovely as Ed had to die.
Oh Ed, we all miss you – you live in our heart
For love cannot die, though death us do part.

(6–8 April 2006)

Chapter 5

Home-Coming

Heather's mislaid passport was recovered from the taxi at Beirut Airport, at the cheap price of a $40 taxi fare, and we caught the early morning Beirut-Heathrow flight on Saturday 8 April, less than 36 hours after our arrival, without further incident. Having ensured that we were in adjacent seats – unlike our outward journey we could not bear to sit apart – we clung to each other during our return flight. We were met at Heathrow by Sarah, the younger of Eddie's sisters, her husband Tim, and Tim's mother who herself had lost a brother in a plane accident some years earlier. Our tearful reunion was for her a painful reminder of that earlier tragedy.

We were surprised to find scores of condolence cards, letters, emails and flowers on our arrival at our Hereford home on the Saturday afternoon, even though it was less than two days since we ourselves had heard of Eddie's death – such is the pace of modern communication. These – together with visits from our friends and neighbours, the cathedral clergy, the local vicar and some of Eddie's closest friends – were added to hour by hour over the coming days so that our downstairs rooms came to resemble a flower shop and card boutique. We even had to ask our painter and decorator to prise open the French windows, so overwhelming was the scent from the flowers. And, three months after the funeral, the last of the orchids from the President of the

Oxford Union still continued to bloom; and at that time we were occasionally receiving letters of condolence from acquaintances who had only just heard the news of Eddie's passing. The careful reading and re-reading of these messages and displaying of such flowers became an important part of the family routine and a huge source of solace in the days of waiting before the funeral.

Not that we then had too much time on our hands properly to grieve. One of our early concerns was how to manage the news of Eddie's death. Within hours of coming home, a FCO communications officer informed us that the press had got hold of the story, which was almost immediately confirmed by one or two of Eddie's friends. In my pre-retirement life I had been used to dealing with the media, but in these circumstances I was utterly relieved to hand things over to Richard Edwards, a former pupil and now a brilliant young journalist, who became our press officer. Richard issued a statement on our behalf (and subsequently prepared an obituary notice) and this became the basis for the reports in the *Daily Telegraph* and other nationals, as well as the front page news story in the *Hereford Times* of 13 April 2006. The 'Tragedy Strikes' banner head-line of the latter journal was made even more poignant by the by-line: 'Families hit by deaths of two brilliant young men'. For Clive Weston, a classical scholar and barrister and also an Old Herefordian, had died, aged 37, just three days after Edward.

There could be no funeral without Eddie's home-coming, and our most immediate concern was to get his body repatriated at the earliest possible moment. Over the next few days that task caused us great anxiety. The difficulties in the way of early repatriation were considerable. 'The Day of the Prophets' holiday in Lebanon on 10 April, the Monday following our return, meant that most of Beirut shut down that day; the Easter weekend a few days later was a potential cause of delay at this end. This gave us a short 'window' of four days for all the paperwork to be completed, if Eddie was to be returned to us before Easter, as was our fervent

wish. Moreover, the bureaucratic obstacles before repatriation could take place, were formidable; we were told that
the police and coroner's reports on Eddie's death had to be
passed through several Lebanese government departments,
and then signed by the mayor of Beirut, before Eddie's body
could be released. That these were overcome so quickly was
due in large measure to the tireless work at the British
Embassy by Trudy Curry and Louise Burrett, with whom
we were in daily contact, and to our elder son, Michael,
who undertook the negotiations with the local insurance
brokers (who again could not have been more helpful) and
the international insurance company. It was a huge relief to
the whole family when we were informed by Chris Long,
the coroner's officer in Hereford, that Eddie had at last
come home to rest for the final time, one week after our
own return. It was Easter Eve.

Meanwhile, we had been busy planning Eddie's funeral,
although we were then uncertain as to its exact date. Given
our, and not least Eddie's, close association for nearly 20
years with Hereford Cathedral, a building Eddie had loved
and one where he had spent a good deal of time during his
formative years, there was only one possible place where
the funeral could have been held. As was said later at his
funeral: 'Ed knew well the space around us here – indeed
he once stood there [at the Tower crossing] and gave a
wickedly convincing impersonation of his school's chaplain.
Here he walked as crucifer; here he read publicly from the
scriptures; here he knelt as communicant'. Nor had we or
our other children any doubts as to the nature of the service,
for we all felt that it should be a full celebration of a life
well lived, rather than a private occasion, and a service for
his friends as well as his family. In this we were blessed by
the full support of the Dean and Precentor, who gave us the
freedom to organise the funeral as we wished.

Having vowed that all five of us should be actively
involved in the service, we also resolved that Eddie's diary
should form the central part of Clare's and Michael's
addresses at the funeral. Sarah would read that uplifting

passage from Romans 8, beginning : 'I am sure that neither death, nor life, nor angels, nor principalities, nor things to come, nor powers, nor height, nor depth, nor anything else in all creation will be able to separate us from the love of God..' Heather determined to tell the story of Eddie's Christian walk and Howard that of his secular journey. We also wanted a sermon and there could be no-one better fitted to undertake that task the Andrew Law, school chaplain during Eddie's teenage years, family friend and our one-time next door neighbour. Andrew readily agreed.

Eddie's Beirut diary also provided clues as to the nature of the music. We knew that he enjoyed rousing hymns, a point emphasised – as we have seen – by his journal entry for Sunday 12 February, when he had compared the songs sung (albeit enthusiastically) at the French Catholic church in Jounieh unfavourably with the hymns 'in our wonderful English tradition'. Accordingly, we chose four family favourites with powerful tunes – 'Tell out My Soul', 'Guide Me O Thou Great Redeemer', 'Love Divine' and 'Thine Be the Glory' – together with 'I am the Bread of Life' which had so helped Heather on that dreadful first night in Beirut. We were less certain about what other music to include until we remembered two further diary entries. The first was for 4 February, when Eddie mentioned 'plugging himself in' 'full blast' to his favourite Mozart aria. Fortunately, he had recorded that it was track no 7 on his CD player. This turned out to have been that romantic aria from *The Magic Flute* that I, too, had once sung for an audition long before Eddie was born. The second musical entry in his journal was even more poignant for on 11 February, again bopping to his CD player on his Jounieh balcony, and having listened to Take That's 'Back for Good', Eddie (and he was not even engaged) had written:

Then, after adopting a suitably grandiose 3-tenors pose, I mouthed along to Bocelli singing 'Time to say Good-bye', gesturing suitably passionately at the right moments and especially at the climax. I have decided, as of last month, that as my new wife and I take our leave from our evening wedding reception, my friends Corinne Hart and Matthew Pochin are going to have to be singing this wonderful tune for us all.

As 'Time to say Good-bye' could not now be sung as he and his bride departed from their wedding reception, we determined that it should be sung at his funeral. Finally, we chose George Herbert's 'Easter' poem, 'Rise, heart, thy Lord is risen'; Bishop Timothy Dudley Smith's version of Psalm 121, 'I lift my eyes to the quiet hills'; and the African-American spiritual 'Steal away to Jesus' as the choir items to complete the musical side of the service.

We were again fortunate in the no small matter of putting the music together within a few days, in being able to call upon the services of our good friend John Williams, one of the best and most experienced directors of music of any school in the country. Despite it having been John's final Easter holiday before his retirement that summer, he embraced our suggestions with his usual enthusiasm. Over the coming days, he gathered a choir of some 50 students of past and present members of the Cathedral School chamber and male-voice choir (of which Eddie had been a founder member), together with one or two from the St John's chapel choir and Simon Sherwood, our gifted son-in-law, and John Seymour, who had trained that first male voice choir. We were blessed, too, in having support from other professional musicians: Martyn Lane, Eddie's former piano teacher, who agreed to play the organ; Jeremy Crowhurst, a cathedral lay clerk and HCS teacher, who (unlike Eddie, as he himself had admitted in his diary) could do full justice to the Mozart aria; and Seb Field, Corinne Hart and Matthew Pochin, who were all willing to sing in their friend's memory.

The question of arranging a suitable time for the funeral posed a particular problem. An earlier rather than a later date was our strong preference. However, given the need for a proper post-mortem and a public announcement in the

Hereford Times, and all the arrangements that still had to be made for the funeral, reception and burial, it became clear that the funeral director was right in claiming that Saturday 22 April – two weeks after our return from Beirut, and one week following Eddie's repatriation – was the earliest and best possible date, even though this meant that the burial could not take place until the following Monday.

We saw Eddie, now decently laid to rest in the chapel at Hereford Hospital, for the last time on Easter Day 2006. Unlike our previous meeting in Beirut, we now had the time and the solitude to tell him all the things we needed to say at our final meeting in this world – things like how much we loved him and what a wonderful son he had been to us – although we forgot to mention that his death had been reported on page 2 of the *Daily Telegraph* ('Torygraph' as he had called it), something that he would have been pleased to have known. The post-mortem duly occurred on Easter Tuesday. Permission was then granted for Eddie's body to be released, which enabled us to confirm in the *Hereford Times* and by email that the funeral would take place on the following Saturday and that it would indeed also be a service of thanksgiving and open to all. We expressed the hope that as many of his friends as possible would be able to attend, expecting that there would be a congregation of perhaps 200 or at the most 300 mourners. As it turned out, however, more than double those numbers, including almost all of Eddie's school year-group and many of his Oxford friends, packed the nave, transepts and choir of Hereford Cathedral on that day. We could not have wished for a better tribute.

On that windswept spring morning, we walked the mile or so to the funeral the long way round, along the banks of the Wye, arm in arm, together with Clare and Simon, Michael and Frances, and Sarah and Tim. The Dean of Hereford, Michael Tavinor, was there at the North Porch to greet us. He was accompanied by his two immediate predecessors – Peter Haynes and Robert Willis – the first time the three Deans had been present together at a service in the cathedral. Andrew Law, Liz Carmichael, the chaplain of St John's who was to sprinkle the coffin with holy water form the Jordan, and Fr Nick King, Eddie's 'Jesuit confessor' and cricketing friend, were all robed and formed part of the procession. We followed them in to the strains of 'Tell out, my soul, the greatness of the Lord', accompanied for the penultimate time by Eddie and the pall-bearers.

We have spoken in Hereford Cathedral many hundreds of times but there is no doubt that this occasion was the hardest for us both, as it was for Clare, Michael and Sarah. Equally it is clear that God gave us the strength to accomplish our addresses (together with some good advice from the Dean to breathe deeply) and get through the funeral service without breaking down, despite the heart-rending circumstances and the duration of the service which lasted over one and a half hours. Afterwards, a friend was kind enough to remark that those 100 minutes had seemed like thirty so uplifted had she been by the occasion. Others wrote in a similar vein of the 'wonderful', 'perfect', 'fitting', 'deeply moving', 'inspiring' and 'most beautiful of services', 'which gave so many of the people who knew and loved him a chance to come together and remember' and 'will stay long in the memory'. But among the most moving tributes were these:

I shall never forget Ed's service: the huge congregation ... the music, 'Steal Away', so generously put together and so expressively and professionally performed, and the soaring voices of Corinne and Matthew; the Beirut journals which gave a rounded personal picture of the author and really brought him among us ...

When the sun came up [on] the morning of Ed's service, the grief I felt for you was so mournful, but the beautiful service and your words were eternally victorious, even if you only felt despair ...

The service was so full of hope and a tangible sense of heaven and earth being very close ...

Yesterday was the most dignified, optimistic and uplifting
funeral of a young person that we have been to ...

I feel I just have to write to let you know what a moving
occasion yesterday's service was. It moved me in quite an
unexpected way from tearful sadness at the beginning to an
uplifting of the spirits, having witnessed...the courage and
unity of your entire family, bonded not only in grief but in
God's love in both sad and happy times...

Had Ed lived to be ... Prime Minister ... He could not
have been honoured any more or better than in that beautiful service – a real testimony to a remarkable boy and to a
very special family ...

Like Eddie I have had a wonderful, privileged and happy
life. If anything happened, I would want my parents to know
that they had blessed me with a rich and fulfilling life that
has been a joy to live. I'm sure Eddie would want you to
know the same, and the service reflected that without, for a
moment, losing any of its poignancy ...

As we came out into brilliant sunshine, another of his
friends said: 'The clouds have parted for Eddie'.

Heather kissed the coffin as it departed to a chapel of rest,
to await the end of the weekend for the Monday burial, and
we left the Close to host a reception for hundreds of relatives and friends at the Cathedral Junior School. Although
given the delayed burial, we had approached Eddie's wake
with some trepidation, it proved to be a joyful occasion. We
had set up a photographic exhibition of his life, from the
day before he was born – featuring Heather and her enormous bump, on her bicycle at Wellington College, with
Michael on the cross-bar, Sarah on the seat behind and
Clare standing beside them – to the last photograph we had
of him, with Michael holding aloft our granddaughter
Esther's toy lamb, taken at a family party the month before
he had left for Beirut. There was a large pedestal flower
display, interlaced with Eddie's school, sporting, debating
and Union ties. Three or four friends, one of whom had
travelled down to Edinburgh that morning, provided the
music, and the wine flowed. It was good to talk about Eddie

and re-live happy memories, among his many friends. One school chum remarked: 'It is just like after our final speech day, with one person missing'.

The contrast between that celebration of a life well-lived and Eddie's burial at a grey Hereford Cemetery on the following Monday morning, in many ways could not have been more stark. Andrew conducted the service with great dignity, and before the committal read these words from the Book of Wisdom:

> The virtuous man, though he die before his time, will find rest. Length of days is not what makes age honourable, nor the number of years the true measure of life; understanding, this is man's grey hairs, untarnished life, this is old age.

These sentiments, which now appear on Eddie's gravestone, provided the link between the Saturday thanksgiving and the Monday burial.

Eddie had finally come home to rest in the city where he had spent much of his life; that Promised Land which he had hoped he might one day represent in Parliament. That ambition had been unfulfilled, but despite the agony, we were (and remain) convinced that it had now been superseded by a more immediate and an infinitely more glorious reality.

Ed's Funeral – One Year On.

A year ago today, the Cathedral church was filled,
  Filled with our mourning and tears.
A year ago today, the Cathedral church was filled,
  Filled with our memories and tears.
A year ago today, the Cathedral church was filled,
  Filled with our sorrow and tears.
Not surprising dear Ed, that now you are dead,
  We all filled the church with our tears.

A year ago today, the Cathedral church was filled,
    Filled with our prayers and our praises.
A year ago today, the Cathedral church was filled,
    Filled with God's word and our praises.
A year ago today, the Cathedral church was filled,
    Filled with our stories and praises.
What a tribute, dear Ed, that though you are dead,
    We still filled the church with God's praises.

A year ago today, the Cathedral church was filled,
    Filled with great music and laughter.
A year ago today, the Cathedral church was filled,
    Filled up with people and laughter.
A year ago today, our grieving hearts were filled,
    Filled with deep fondness and laughter.
What a tribute, dear Ed, that though you are dead
    We still fill the world with our laughter.

(22 April 2007)

Chapter 6

Commemorations

As it turned out, the funeral service of thanksgiving was only the beginning of the Eddie commemorations. At the start of the summer term, prayers were said and silences held at Abberley and Hereford Cathedral School. At St John's chapel, Oxford, on the feast day of St Mark the evangelist, Eddie was remembered by Fr Nick as he presided over the termly Catholic mass which Eddie used to attend when he could. Fr. Nick ended his brilliant address:

> As we reflect on these several stories [of Ed's death, Easter, St Mark and St John's 'catholic community'] we ... have to think about what life can possibly mean in the light of its precariousness; and we must decide what are the values by which we shall live, and then live them out with cheerful courage. If we do that we shall appropriately honour the memory of Edward Tomlinson, and at the same time appropriately celebrate the Easter that is at the heart of Christian faith.

This was one of a number of masses, from Beirut to Bath, remembering Eddie – all of which had been requested by catholic friends and relatives. Other friends planted a tree in the Holy Land in his memory.

Then, towards the end of that summer term, a memorial service for Eddie was held in St John's chapel, attended by many of his student friends. Four of them – Jonathan

McDonagh, Haris Theodorelis-Rigas, Richard Tydeman and
Quentin Williams – gave addresses stressing different aspects
of their friendship. Thomas Goodhead, Eddie's debating
partner, read that evocative passage from Revelation 21: 'I
saw a new heaven and a new earth ... This is the victor's
heritage', and Fr Nick again spoke, confidently asserting that
Eddie lives on and that 'we shall be one day reunited in the
Triune God whom he served and longed for'. David
Baskeyfield, the former organ scholar at St John's, whom
Eddie had hired to play at his drinks parties during his presidential term, came back to play the organ, and the chapel
choir led the music, starting with Parry's anthem, 'My soul,
there is a country', and including three rousing hymns –
'Now is eternal life', 'Now thank we all our God', and (as at
the funeral) 'Guide me, O Thou Great Redeemer'. Eddie
would have loved it.

Ed would also have appreciated the secular commemorations
by friends from HCS and Oxford. On the day of the funeral,
the school male voice choir, on tour in Ireland, gave a concert
in St Patrick's Cathedral, Dublin, and dedicated it to his memory. Towards the end of that summer term, a memorial cricket match was held at the school playing field between the 1st
XI and the Old Boys – won by the school off the last ball of
the day, with Michael appropriately taking 6 wickets, his best
return at Wyeside; and at Speech Day an Edward Tomlinson
memorial debating prize was awarded for the first time in 2006.
During that summer's Three Choirs Festival, at a fringe event,
Kaloi k'Agathoi put on three workshops on Aristophanes' comedy, pending the 2007 production of *Clouds*.

At Oxford, tributes were made at the Union by Tom
Goodhead and Matthew Richardson, erstwhile Librarian,
and other friends, and a minute's silence kept at the first
debate of the Summer Term 2006. A month later, two
further cricket matches were held at the St John's ground
where Eddie had enjoyed so many summer afternoons. The
students had clubbed together to buy a bench bearing a
plaque engraved with his name and highest score (118*
versus the Law Society) – a suitable memorial giving his

propensity for 'lounging' if not 'loafing'. Heather also baked two cakes for the occasion, one featuring a model of 'Excalibur', Eddie's cricket bat, decorated with the words: 'Edward/Excelled at/Clobbering/A/Lot of /Illustrious/Boundaries with/Undisguised/Relish'; the other had these words emblazoned: 'Edward/Delightedly/Whacked all balls/Abhorring the/Rigour of/Defence'.

In between, we determined to attend the degree ceremony in the Sheldonian Theatre at Oxford, where Eddie's degree was awarded posthumously. The citation read: 'This is to certify that Edward Alexander Tomlinson, St John's College, satisfied the examiners in the Final Honour School of *Literae Humaniores* on 5 July 2005, and was placed by them in the Second Class, Division One, [and] would, but for his death, have been admitted to the degree of Bachelor of Arts on 6 May 2006'. We managed to stay for the first part of the ceremony, until Eddie's name was read out, and then quietly departed the scene. At the St John's party following the graduation, we met another grieving mother and father, whose son had also died between his final exams and the awarding of the degree. A minute's silence was called for by the President of the college and held for them both. Later that summer, St John's again remembered them at a college 'gaudy'. 'Let this feast, then,' the Orator proclaimed, 'be dedicated to their memory; in our enjoyment and appreciation of the evening we will be offering them the best possible tribute'. (*Consecretur quidem, si vobis placet, hoc convivium memoriae eorum; gaudio enim laudibusque iuivenes animosos decentissime possumus honorare.*) Eddie would undoubtedly have seconded that motion – and maybe in Latin as well.

More recently, there have been other commemorations. The most public was Liz Grice's article ('In his short life he made a difference') published in the *Daily Telegraph* during the Lebanese invasion, about six months after Ed's death. We had originally wanted to see Ed's Beirut journal published, rather than a feature article with a large mournful photograph of us, but at least Liz managed to include a

number of diary extracts and wrote a very sensitive piece
which captured Ed's spirit and told the story of our early
grief. Friends have told us how moved they were by the
article, and what a splendid tribute it was.

The memorial debate at the Oxford Union in January
2007, initiated by Laura Poots – Ed's former girl-friend and
herself the Union President for Hilary Term 2005 – was an
even more fitting tribute. Laura decided that it would be
appropriate to repeat 'The Future is Blue' debate, one of the
motions from Eddie's own presidential term. Four prominent
politicians – Michael Howard, David Lammy, Clare Short
and Ed Vaizey – together with Tom Goodhead and Chris
Deutsch OH, former chairman of the Cathedral School
debating society and now an Oxford student, kindly agreed
to be the platform speakers. Ed's three officers for Hilary
Term 2004 also came back for the debate. Following a splendid dinner in the Macmillan Hall, we entered a crowded
chamber to the customary slow hand-clap. Theo Roos, that
term's President, then invited me to chair the debate, and Ed's
officers to resume their former seats on the platform. There
was thunderous applause as we did so, and I just about
managed to hang on to my emotions as I sat down in the
same presidential chair that Ed had occupied three years
earlier. I opened the debate by speaking of Ed's love for
debating, and said something about how he had won 10
successive elections at Oxford (for OUCA and Union positions) before gaining the presidency – despite falling on his
sword after one of them for alleged electoral malpractice!
The debate then proceeded without incident, Michael
Howard being at his coruscating best, and Clare Short nearly
swinging the House ('the future is not blue, it's not red ... it
must be green') with a barn-storming final speech. But the
most moving contribution was from the floor by Mark
Higgins, a blind lawyer and one of Ed's friends, who argued
passionately against the government's closure of special
schools. Appropriately, the motion was carried by a handful
of votes.

Reuben Edward Compton in the capable hands of Michael
Howard and Clare Short, with other admirers, at the Oxford
Union memorial debate, January 2007

The Edward Tomlinson Memorial Debate

A grand celebration of Eddie's short life
Was held at the Union today.
We were touched to the core that so many were there
And to hear what they all had to say.

There were friends from his college, friends from his school,
All with their stories to tell;
Friends from the Union, his cricket team, too,
And friends of his family as well.

The chatter was great as we gathered for drinks
And met the guest speakers who came,
Eminent MPs abandoned the House,
In order to honour Ed's name.

At dinner we listened to many a tale
Of Ed's driving all over the States,
The places he saw, the things that he did –
In addition to winning debates!

Then we crossed to the chamber. The motion proposed,
'That the future shall surely be blue'.
There was thunderous applause as H took Eddie's seat
To preside and see matters through.

The evening was opened by Eddie's friend Tom,
Followed by Chris Deutsch from School.
The Tory, Ed Vaizey, spoke next with panache
And Dave Lammy showed Britain is 'cool'.

From the floor there were speeches of varying hue,
The best from Ed's blind friend called Mark,
His points made an impact on all who were there
We all had to sit up and hark.

Then came the big guns – Michael and Clare,
To round off the evening's debate.
Michael was smooth and moved with great grace
While Clare spoke with passion innate.

The evening's debate was clearly good fun,
But hugely emotional, too,
For each speech had a preface about our young Ed,
Respect and affection shone through.

The tributes were touching; it made us feel proud
Of Edward, our dearly loved son.
A great inspiration, a really good friend,
A thinker, a doer, and fun!

Our pride though, with sadness is deeply entwined,
And his death has quite shattered our hearts.
For Eddie so loving, so warm and so true
Was much more than the sum of his parts.

Dear Ed, you'd have loved it! We wish you'd been there!
Did you look down from heaven and see
Your old Dad presiding, your young nephew, too,
Your brother, your sisters and me?

We were humbled to hear of the promise you held,
In the eyes of all those you knew.
But for us, darling Ed, it's the *person* we miss,
The genuine article, YOU!

(24 January 2007)

Eddie's Hereford friends, too, wished to perform *Clouds* as
(in Nico Vaughan's words) 'a fitting tribute to the fun, inspi-
rational and undeniably memorable Eddie T'. In early
September 2007, a toga party – he was 'most comfortable in
a toga', according to the charity auction catalogue! – held at
the Hereford Shirehall launched the production and raised
over £2000 for two charities. These were the Primary Club, a
cricketers' charity much loved and supported by Ed from his
early teens; and CO Gas Safety, chosen by us as it raises
awareness of carbon monoxide poisoning. Heather's heart-
felt speech at the party was a great commemoration in itself.
It was addressed to Alex Outhwaite, the show's producer, but
applied to all those involved in the production:

> Alex, there are not words to express how very touched
> Howard and I and the whole family are that you are going
> to all this trouble for Ed, so-to-speak. I'm sure he's ever so
> pleased! He really did love Kaloi k'Agathoi and all it stands
> for, and he had a huge amount of fun playing his part in its
> early life and development. He must have driven you to
> distraction as he was not easily directed.
>   Our elder daughter, Clare, would vouch for this. When the
> family was young, Clare used to write and direct dramas for
> the children to act in. Often adult neighbours were invited
> into our garden to watch these extravaganzas. From the age
> of two, Ed was drafted in to play usually minor roles, such
> as 'the maid'. Ed was utterly infuriating as he would do
> exactly what he wanted, rather than what had been

rehearsed, and when he tired of doing even his version, he would just amble off. He could neither be coaxed nor bullied back again. So even as a little boy he was not easy to direct, Alex, and when he eventually turned up (late, as ever) for your rehearsals, we know that he tended to slip in his own ideas, whether you wanted them or not!

Alex, soon after Ed's death, you and the KK gang put together a few examples of just these very things – for example, the yogurt drinking, cricket playing Herakles, in *The Frogs*. I'm sure you'll never forget the memorable lyrics:

'Would you bat if I asked you to bat? Would you walk if someone cried howzat? Would you bowl with one over to go, down the front, line and leg, for me? I can be your Herakles, baby. (Doo doo doo doo) I can kiss away the pain. (Doo doo doo doo) I could play like this for ever. (Doo doo doo) Just please don't take my kebab away. (Whispered) Let Herakles be your hero baby.'

Or the production of *The Assembly Women*, which preceded and possibly inspired the later formation of KK, where Ed dressed in a sharp tux in his role as the company pianist, but was wearing nothing but boxer shorts from the waist down. I expect many people here could add their own personal favourites, but I won't go on. Ed loved every moment of it, Alex. He had such fun, and that was what he loved best. Thank you for all those happy times; thank you for all that has been organized for tonight's launch; thank you for finishing off and up-dating Ed's script for *Clouds*. We can't wait to see the performances! And thank you for making this a toga party – one of Ed's top favourite things. I'm sure he's beaming down his approval on all of us now. Thank you, and well done!

The launch was followed by five performances in Abergavenny, London and Hereford. The show – a raucous musical adaptation of Aristophanes' original satire on education – played to full houses, which included many of Ed's friends. A further wonderful tribute (particularly alluding, I seem to remember, to one of Eddie's rudest but most memorable lines) was paid to him by Louis Fonseca (who played 'Righteous'), after the final run. Eddie had translated about half the play before his death, and through the first half of the show we could hear much of his voice. We heard him not least in the political jokes and the references to 'The Zeus Delusion', 'Plaid Attica' and the 'Nebulous Creed', based on the 'Nicene Creed' from the Book of Common Prayer which we had found transcribed on Ed's Beirut note-paper. As the *Hereford Times* put it:

> Striving to produce a show that was the best possible, the phrase 'It's what Eddie would have wanted' (*Id quod voluis-set Edwardus*), was heard frequently, and it's a phrase that has become something of a motto for the company.

Clouds

On Ed's birthday cake I wrote:
'Ed's Clouds
Ed beyond the clouds
Ed in our heart ...
Always'

Ed's 'Clouds' was something different,
Quite close to the original, we're told,
By Aristophanes.
But Ed's 'Clouds' was something different.

You could say a translation
Adaptation, up-dating, rewriting
A collaborative effort – all true
But Ed's 'Clouds' was something different.

Ed's 'Clouds' – not just a performance;
More of a celebration, a tribute.
Hearing his words, reliving his humour, Ed almost tangible
Yes, Ed's 'Clouds' was something different.

So why were they poignant, our laughter and pleasure?
Why was there pain and sadness entwined?
Why did we weep, though finding it funny?
Because Ed's 'Clouds' is something different,
Now that Ed's dead.
(Reflecting on 26 October 2007)

And then there have been further Cathedral memorials which were unexpected. Unbeknown to us, a close friend generously enabled Edward's name to be commemorated, in perpetuity, in the Cathedral as a part of the beautiful new shrine to St Ethelbert, Hereford Cathedral's patron saint, which tells the story of the saint's (and king's) life in 13 brilliantly coloured panels. After some consideration, and with the help of the Dean and Siobhan de Souza, we decided on this Latin variation of the Book of Wisdom verse from Ed's gravestone: *Vita non annis computanda sed factis.* These words are inscribed under a panel that depicts the death of the young king in 794. At the service of dedication on 9 June 2007, and following the prayers before the shrine at the east end of the altar, where we prayed for Ed and other departed friends, 'giving thanks for their lives and commending them to the loving mercy of God', I lit one of the shrine's candles, a symbol of the hope of resurrection for Ed and all the saints. Five months later, came a further memorial, with the Dean's dedication of the new Sunday school piano in memory of Edward (as well as Venetia, a Sunday school teacher who had recently died). The Dean's playing of Schumann's 'Dreaming' before the service on All Saints' Sunday could not have been more appropriate.

This St Ethelbert service had coincided with the 75th anniversary of the Friends of Hereford Cathedral, and later during this anniversary year I was also invited to give the Friends annual autumn lecture, which at the secretary's kind suggestion was named 'The Edward Tomlinson Memorial Lecture'. I had spent some months researching the life of Sarah Alston, fourth Duchess of Somerset, a seventeenth century heiress and a generous benefactor to Hereford

Cathedral School, so a lecture associating her name with Edward's seemed fitting. I prefaced my talk with these words:

> It has to be said that Eddie was not a natural lecture-goer – I never quite discovered how many lectures he actually attended during his five years at Oxford (not many, I suspect!) – but as a gifted linguist and story-teller, he was a natural historian ... And as a proud Old Herefordian, a former member of Somerset House and someone who had an interest in the School's history ... I think Eddie would have approved of the subject matter of tonight's talk. Who knows, had he attended, he might even have enjoyed the lecture?

Such are the public commemorations to date. Family and friends have given generously in Ed's name to various charities – the Primary Club, BODS (a Herefordshire outdoor educational charity), the Oxford Union memorial prize, the Hereford Cathedral Close project, the Carbon Monoxide safety campaign and the Middle East appeal (following the 2006 Gaza/Lebanon invasion). It is wonderful beyond words that so many people have wanted to remember Ed in so many different ways. We are deeply grateful to everyone who has played any part in these events. What a special place Ed must have had (and has) in their hearts! Each occasion, in a sense, has brought him back to life; yet each has sharpened our loss and reinforced the fact that our lovely Eddie is no longer with us. Countless tears have been shed on every occasion; each has left us more drained of emotional reserves. Yet, given that we could not have him back with us, we would not have had it otherwise.

Chapter 7

The Inquest

Heather, Clare, Sarah, Paul (our wonderful vicar), together with myself – Michael not being able to make it as he was himself in the middle of a court case – took the same route, by the banks of the Wye, to Eddie's inquest as we had to his funeral: along the tow-path below the old infirmary, over Victoria Bridge, on the Bishop's Meadow path to the Old Bridge and so to the coroner's office in Bridge Street. However, this fine day, Thursday 28 March 2007, had none of the cold 'bite' of the funeral walk. It was a beautiful spring morning, spoilt only by the knowledge that we had to go through a difficult inquiry into our dear son's death, in a distant place, almost one year previously.

It had taken nearly a year to assemble the evidence, such as it was, for the inquest. We were told that this time-lapse was not unusual with deaths abroad; and in Eddie's case the peculiar circumstances of his death and the war in Lebanon the previous summer had made things more complicated. Indeed, we had been asked by Chris Long, Hereford's excellent coroner's officer, whether the coroner should press the Lebanese authorities for more details of the events surrounding Eddie's death, which would have again delayed proceedings. We both agreed that further delay would have been pointless. As it was, the photographs of the shower unit in Eddie's room, and the further investigation of the gas supply in the hostel, both of which had been requested by

Hereford's coroner, had done little to clarify the events of that tragic night of the 4th/5th April 2006. Moreover, the shower unit had already been removed from room 14, following the Deputy Ambassador's visit to the hostel the previous May. It was clear that the evidence, unsatisfactory as it was, was as complete as it was going to get.

It was our first experience of a coroner's court, although Chris Long had taken us through the likely procedure. Sadly, he was not able to greet us: his wife had been involved in a serious car smash that very day, a salutary reminder that unforeseen accidents are not simply confined to unstable Middle Eastern countries. However, to our great good fortune, we were accompanied by Chris and Lynne Poole, who had been with us on that first dreadful day in Beirut and, following their retirement to Herefordshire, had kindly agreed to be at our side at this journey's end. Three journalists also accompanied us, so with Chris's deputy and the coroner himself, a party of 12 crowded into the small library of that solicitor's office. Extra chairs had to be found. It seemed more like an intimate governors' meeting than a formal court hearing, except that the subject matter was far more serious than any board that we had ever attended.

But Chris had prepared us well for the event. We had been shown the Lebanese documentary evidence – headed 'Investigation about finding the British citizen Tomlinson dead by fate in Jounieh' (thereby revealing the Muslim belief that one's fate is written in advance, and that it was Ed's 'kismet' to die when he did, a belief we find impossible to share) – and until the end of the proceedings there were no surprises. The coroner, in a dispassionate voice, read out statements from the key officers and witnesses: those from Lebanon – the police reports, the initial findings of the Beirut pathologist and the accounts of witnesses from the hotel – and the statements of the Home Office pathologist, forensic toxicologist and the Vice Consul at the British Embassy in Beirut. From these sources, the story of Edward's last hours, the discovery of his body and the causes of his death can be reconstructed.

Ed had moved into the St Joseph Hotel from the Apostles School at Jounieh on the afternoon of 1 April 2006, saying that he intended to stay there for about two weeks before moving on to a larger apartment. Maria Lizane, the hostel manager, was the last person to see him alive – some three days later on the late evening of 4 April.

Tragically, Maria was soon to be a witness of a very different kind, for not having seen Edward for two days, she opened his room with her spare key at about 11am on 6 April, only to find him lying motionless on the bed with blood traces on his face. Having informed Abdullah Al Chaer, her supervisor, Maria again tried several times to wake Ed. She then called Red Cross officers – the supervisor thinking that Edward might have been suffering from an illness – who pronounced him dead. By 1pm the Red Cross had informed the internal security forces, and staff adjutant Sefian Taleb and staff sergeant Georges Francis immediately went to the premises. Inside room 14, they found 'a man in his twenties, lying on the bed, in stiffness state, some blood on his nose and face, the odour of the corpse [being] ... strong'. There was no 'scattering of things in the room' or other evidence of violence and 'the dead man was still wearing his bed clothes'. The General Attorney of Appeal in Mount Lebanon was then informed and he ordered the duty pathologist to examine the body and the police to continue their investigations. The British Embassy was also contacted and the death site secured. At 2.15, a patrol from the 'accidents bureau at Baabda [Hospital]' started to carry out their survey and less than half an hour later the pathologist, Dr Elias Khoury, arrived to examine Edward's body. At 5.30, two hours before our touch-down, it was transported to the morgue of Baabda Hospital. The room was then closed and statements taken from the supervisor, manager and one of the residents.

Dr Khoury's report was quoted at some length during the inquest. He confirmed that he had found 'no trace of blood, weapon, medicine or anything strange' in the infamous room 14. The room was 'neat and clean', although (ominously as it turned out) there was water on the floor of the adjacent shower, and when the hot water was turned on 'I smelled a gas odour for a while and then it disappeared'. He also identified 'an interrupted pinky colour' on Edward's back as 'occurs in case of poisoning by CO', but having eliminated the possibility of a heart failure, he initially diagnosed 'a brain electric shock' akin to epilepsy (partly from the evidence of the clenched teeth), as the cause of death. He reiterated that the death had occurred 'without violence or resistance' and that its cause was 'strictly clinical'. The time of death was estimated to have been more than 48 hours earlier, and was put at some time during the previous Tuesday night and the early hours of the Wednesday morning. Although it was subsequently proved to have been an incorrect diagnosis, in the circumstances Dr Khoury had conducted a thoroughly professional investigation into the nature of Edward's death.

As Dr Khoury had foreseen, a full autopsy was needed to 'inform us with precision' about what had happened to Edward. This was provided by the post-mortem and blood test reports of the British medical scientists, Dr Tapp, a Home Office pathologist, and Dr Elliott, a forensic toxicologist. Their investigations later revealed that Edward's post-mortem blood contained carboxyhaemoglobin (COHb) saturation of 53%, a level in excess of the 30% saturation which was often found in cases of fatal fume exposure caused by fire and at least double the level of some car suicides. There was no other evidence either of natural disease in Edward's body or of anything else untoward in his blood. A 53% COHb saturation was sufficiently high to have been the sole cause of Edward's death.

The Hereford Coroner recognised this when he recorded that Edward had died on 5 April 2006 in room 14 of St Joseph's Hotel, Jounieh, of carbon monoxide poisoning. Given that we had had access to all the statements, this formal recording of the cause of death came as no surprise, although we had been devastated some months earlier when we had first learned the result of the blood test which proved that Edward had not died of some kind of seizure. However, we were not in the least prepared for the coroner's recorded verdict. Having reviewed the evidence and ruled out the possibilities of natural causes and suicide, three options remained: unlawful killing, accidental death or an open verdict. We made the assumption that the coroner would decide on one of the latter two alternatives. How wrong we were.

Following the blood test findings, the British Ambassador had recommended that the Lebanese authorities undertake 'a very urgent investigation into possible sources of carbon monoxide at the hotel'. Consequently, Mr Al Chaer, the supervisor, made a further statement to the police expressing his surprise that Edward had been poisoned in this way. He claimed that less than a year previously some hotel rooms had been equipped with new French made water-heaters and that 'there is no way that they can leak gas', the gas bottles having been put outside the rooms. He admitted, however, that 'Edward might have inhaled this substance as a result of closing all the outlets of the room tightly and using hot water excessively'. Nevertheless, he undertook 'to immediately remove' the equipment 'so that such an incident does not recur with other hotel guests'. Chris Poole later confirmed that this had been done, the manager suggesting that it had been tested by people brought in by the police both before it was renewed and after its re-installation, and that they could find no fault with it. Despite this claim, the British Vice-Consul had written to the editors of the 'Lonely Planet' and 'Footprint' travel guides and they had promised to remove details of the hotel from their future publications.

This evidence, together with the earlier statements and some murky photographs of the water heater and shower unit, were clearly insufficient for a British court. The coroner, while recognising that inquests into deaths abroad were fraught with difficulty, and that matters had been made worse in Edward's case by the intervening hostilities between Lebanon and Israel, pointed out the contradictions. For example, the manager's later claim to Chris Poole that the water-heater in room 14 was the only one of its type in the hotel contradicted the supervisor's second statement to the police of 13 May that other rooms in the hotel had been similarly equipped and that the showers had been used many times without accident. This contradiction was impossible to resolve in the Hereford hearing. There was a further lack of other supporting evidence – for instance, relating to the claim that no fault had been found in the equipment before and after its installation in the kitchen. No tests, moreover, were carried out on the water-heater immediately following Edward's death. Nor was there evidence of its proper installation in the first place or its further maintenance. As the coroner observed, the assumption must be that there was no such evidence.

And so, after an hour or so, the coroner came to his final verdict. Mr Al Chaer's (the hotel supervisor's) possible explanation of Edward's death – through the closure of outlets and excessive use of hot water – was dismissed. It provided no defence and did not absolve him from his duty of safeguarding against an entirely foreseeable accident. The coroner further pointed out that there was no evidence of notices, warning of the need to keep windows open and against the over-use of hot water, having been displayed in or around room 14. He also referred to the initial smell of gas, reported by Dr Khoury, when the water-heater was turned on. To return a verdict of unlawful killing, the coroner explained, he had to find that there was a duty of care owed by someone to Edward; that there was a breach of that 'substantial duty'; and that the breach occurred 'by way of gross neglect'. The coroner had no difficulty in finding against the hotel supervisor on all three counts. He finally pronounced: 'I am satisfied there was gross neglect here and accordingly I return a verdict of unlawful killing'. Although it had been clear for some minutes that he had been working towards this verdict, these cold words came as a profound shock to us all. Although we had by now adjusted (as far as one can ever do so) to the fact that Eddie had not died from natural causes, we had yet to make a further massive mental adjustment – from 'Ed had died accidentally' to 'Ed had been unlawfully killed'.

After a short and informal discussion with the coroner, we had to undergo the ordeal of a press conference with journalists from the *Daily Telegraph* and the *Hereford Times*. We had been prepared for this but realised that the 'unlawful killing' verdict would ensure more extensive publicity than we had anticipated. Our statement, too, would need to be modified for we could hardly now admit that the verdict was 'one that was always likely to have been given'. Nevertheless, our prepared statement about the Beirut investigation – despite its obvious limitations – and our feelings one year on from Eddie's death could be given without amendment and from the heart:

> In the circumstances and given the limited resources, we feel that the Beirut authorities did their best. We were treated with consideration by the Beirut police, the pathologist and manager of the hostel, as well as by the British Embassy who gave us the utmost support at the time of our visit and subsequently.
>
> We are all still devastated by Eddie's tragic death. He was a loving and much loved son, brother and friend and a greatly talented young man who had the world at his feet and everything to live for. He was enjoying life in Beirut, had made lots of friends there and felt great empathy with the Lebanese. As with all such deaths, it is an added sadness that he was in the wrong place at the wrong time. We take comfort from our memories of many happy times together – he was a wonderful son and packed so much into his life – and are sustained by our Christian faith.

I then read out the following message from a friend that we had received just that week – 'May God bless you … and may you know that … your beloved son is in light and joy and peace, fully himself' – and said: 'We believe that to be true'. To the inevitable question: 'Are you going to take any further action?' I answered:

Clearly we are extremely saddened by Edward's death, but we are not angry and hold no personal vendettas. We hope that there will be a tightening of safety practices in hostels to stop anything like this happening again. We also hope that all travellers will be better warned about the dangers of carbon monoxide poisoning.

Within days we were contacted by the chief executive of the charity for carbon monoxide gas safety.

The Inquest

We sit round a table, apprehensive and sad,
in a small, book-lined room.
Concern for each other etched in our faces,
broken hearts aching,
yet still raising a smile of gratitude
to those who join us in this unfamiliar formality –
the inquest into the death of our Ed.

A Coroner's inquest: an ancient procedure
in our society
safe-guards citizens against unexplained deaths.
No longer by quill on parchment
are findings recorded,
but computer and microphone catch every word
as we look into the death of our Ed.

We listen intently to all that is said,
each cold, clinical fact, relayed in translation:
'We were called to the room.
Young man in his twenties,
wearing pyjamas,
hand on his nose,
blood on his face,
body quite stiff,
on his bed,
dead.'

Tears well up, hankies are needed
as we hear about the death of our Ed.

No natural cause had taken Ed from us.
Thoughts of a 'seizure', now are long past.
Carbon monoxide from a duff shower unit
Invisible,
Odourless,
Tasteless,
Silent
Deadly poison
Had caused the death of our Ed.

The Coroner's verdict: unlawfully killed.
Our dear precious Eddie unlawfully killed.
We don't like that verdict: unlawfully killed.
It sounds so much worse: unlawfully killed.
But what can be worse? Our dear Eddie's dead.
It might save another, and that would be good.
We don't want another unlawfully killed.

Lost in thought, downcast, we leave the inquest
and set off for a pub lunch, valiantly chatting,
trying to cheer each other on.
What can be worse than Ed dead?
We all know, though we do not say,
that Ed killed is worse than Ed dead.
Ed killed is very much worse than Ed dead.

People say that life must go on, and it does
regardless of inquests.
The sun still shines, the grass still grows,
the birds are still singing,
though we hardly notice,
much less do we care.
'though we don't begrudge anyone else these joys.

Day follows day.
Newspapers report the inquest's findings.
People nod sympathetically in our direction.
A brave one steps forward and clasps my hand,
head bowed low.
She cannot bear to see the sorrow in my face
or the tears in my eyes.

Words fail her. Words fail us all.
What can anyone say **unless** Easter has meaning
and Jesus was raised?
Our Ed is in heaven, in glory with Christ!
What could be better?
Well, Ed here on earth would be better for **us**,
if I may be so bold.

But that's not an option. So we go on,
grieving for all we have lost,
yet thankful for what we have had,
and thankful for what we have still,
and thankful for what can never be taken away.
We cling to the hope we have in Christ
and recover slowly from the inquest
into the death of our Ed.

(29 March 2007)

Chapter 8

Grieving

How does one come to terms with a loss such as ours? Does one ever do so? Should one? To these questions we can only give partial and limited answers. While not totally agreeing with the New York journalist's observation on the fifth anniversary of September 11 that grief is one of the most powerful emotions but also one of the shortest-lived, what is clear some five months after Eddie's death, is that time tends to heal – even if that healing is imperceptible to oneself – but that it does not occur in a linear way. 'Progress' is infinitely slow and it frequently lapses.

Over the past months, even if we had wanted to do so, it has proved impossible to remove Eddie from our consciousness – or sometimes, when asleep, our sub-consciousness – for more than a few hours. Even now, it is as though he will be coming back home in a day or two prior to the start in October of his Law course. Although it would have been worse in our old house, where Eddie had lived for 18 years, his image – real and imagined – is still everywhere. Before he left for Beirut, it was Eddie who helped arrange the pictures in our new home and his face still beams at us from College, Union and family photographs. Eddie and I had even left a carefully measured space on our dining-room wall – appropriately at the end of the line of similar photographs of Clare, Michael and Sarah – for his graduation portrait, now occupied instead by that of his matriculation.

And we can see Eddie here now, either ruefully tapping on the window to attract our attention to let him in, after he had characteristically forgotten his keys, or punching the air in mock celebration after yet another victory in garden croquet or mowing the grass in his carpet slippers. These are all comfortable spectres.

We also see Eddie in other places, not least in Hereford Cathedral, where he spent so much of his time, arm in arm and in whispered conversation with his mother as he accompanied her to the communion rail. He is still among his friends at the school playing fields and the studio theatre. He is still there on our visits to Oxford – at the Union, his College or the Old Parsonage where we sometimes had tea together. He is with us watching cricket on our visits to Lord's. We are especially reminded of his presence on family occasions – in their homes when a picture provokes a memory and as we throw a ball around on family walks and holidays. We can even hear his voice – 'It's all right, Dad', he had remarked about his new room in the hostel – as that last 3 April telephone conversation is replayed in my mind. Eddie is with us all in our imaginings and yet our lives are incomplete because he is not now here among us. As we work and go about our daily round we muse: 'How Eddie would have loved this!' 'What would Eddie have thought?' 'Eddie could have translated this!' And as we read the lives of the famous or letters from the young grown old, there is always the question of what might have been.

First Anniversary

The anniversary looms of that very sad day,
when Ed died.
Our hearts were quite shattered, our lives blown apart,
when Ed died.
Our minds now relate all we see and we hear
to Ed's life,
Everything round us, the things that we do,
echo Ed's life.

We hear of a youngster cut down in his prime,
        like our Ed,
Bursting with promise which won't be fulfilled,
        like our Ed.
We think of the parents' and siblings' loss too,
        as our loss.
Our hearts break anew for all those who grieve.
        It's our grief.

Howard plays golf and remembers the times
        when Ed came,
He takes out the mower as he used to with Ed,
        for their croquet game.
He puts lunch on the table as he did that first term
        when Ed was here,
He looks round our home, brimful of memories,
        wishing Ed was here.

A French phrase or Arabic we spent evenings learning,
        speak Ed's name.
A piano played *forte*, or oboe that honks,
        speak Ed's name.
A slushy old pop song or fine Mozart aria
        speak Ed's name.
It's just that without our Ed,
        they simply don't sound the same.

We glance at the window where Ed used to knock –
        He'd lost his key!
We see his face beaming there, as he grinned
        his apology.
There sits his penguin mug, a Christmas gift,
        chosen so lovingly.
How my heart dearly yearns to have him back!
        But it is not to be.

Dear Lord, I won't leave it there. I know you care
        infinitely.

I still have a thankful heart. I love you, Lord,
... falteringly.
Give me the grace, I pray, to live each day
in your sufficiency;
Not in self-pity, Lord, but praising your Name, O Lord,
'Til I join Ed in Glory, Lord,
joyfully.

(5 April 2007)

While not wholly subscribing to the 'stages of grief' theory, there has been some pattern to our grieving, even though the patterns are constantly changing in colour and intensity. In our dazed state, on first learning of the news at Beirut Airport, our very first thought was what has Eddie done to be involved with the Lebanese police? It took some moments to realise that what the police had been doing was investigating Eddie's sudden death. Disbelief – or refusal to believe – then occasionally manifested itself in the following weeks, with the thought that Eddie would soon return, even though we had seen photographs of him on his death-bed and had twice identified his body. But shock and numbness were the predominant emotions in those early days, together with feelings of anger – not least with God – and utter powerlessness. God had not saved Eddie; nor could we have done anything to prevent our baby dying alone so far away in a foreign country.

However, this did not prevent us, in our less rational moments, experiencing acute pangs of guilt, a guilt made more intense when it became apparent that Eddie had died of fume poisoning in his Beirut room rather than of a seizure, which could have happened anywhere. Why had we not been able to persuade Eddie to start on his Law course straight away, as had been his original intention, rather than deferring and taking another gap year? Why had we so tamely acquiesced when his plans to go to Tunisia fell through and he announced that he was going to Lebanon? Why had I bought him the Middle East guide 'Lonely Planet' guide-book, which listed the Hotel St

Joseph, and why had we so readily agreed that it would be a good idea for him to move there and not insisted that he stayed at the Foyer, his original accommodation, before moving into more suitable lodgings? As historians, we both knew about the dangers of the unhistorical use of hindsight. We also knew that there were good answers to such questions. Eddie had wanted a break from the exertions of his Oxford years, and felt that after a few months abroad he would return well refreshed and be better able to tackle learning the Law. His knowledge of Arabic and experience of travel might prove useful to his future career in Law and Politics. After weeks of frustration trying to plan a trip to Tunis, doors opened in Lebanon within a matter of days. Hotel St Joseph seemed an ideal place for him to stay (and for us to join him) in Jounieh for a week or two – it was relatively cheap, well written up in the Planet Guide, and Maria could help him with his French. Correspondingly, Ed was getting fed up with the restrictions (and smells!) of the Foyer. In any case, he was pretty stubborn, and while he always listened to our view, nothing we could have said would have altered his decision once his mind was made up. Such logic did not stop our minds repeatedly pondering these, and other, hypothetical 'what ifs?' Above all, latterly, why, despite his extensive education, had he not learned more about the dangers of carbon monoxide poisoning? Our rational minds could not counter the irrationality of our raw emotions during our darker moods.

Our walk away from those times of complete despair has not been achieved without periodic stumbles and retreats. For example, sorting out Eddie's financial and other affairs and the eventual clearing of his room at home – now, at last, in the second year of his death and thanks to Heather's strength and insight, transformed into a bunk-bedded, re-carpeted new bedroom for our grandchildren – were difficult tasks. Even harder was coping with the drip-feed of the suspicion and then the knowledge that Ed had not died of natural causes, and the long wait for the inquest. The war in Lebanon brought unwanted memories flooding back and more pain. We could not bear to see on television all that Ed had feared for the country actually happening before our very eyes. It was like Eddie being in the news daily. We could hardly bear to watch the bulletins yet we had to know what was happening. We renewed contact with the friends that Ed had made in Lebanon and with Maria, the manageress of the hostel. We wanted to know that they were safe. How we wished that Ed was alive to be worried about!

More frequently, our lapses into grief have been triggered unexpectedly – by the chance discovery of his Beirut luggage label when we were using Eddie's new suitcase for the first time; or being reminded of Ed's baby-hood by the antics of a toddler – like Ed, the youngest in a family of four – in the cathedral; or by an oboe (one of Ed's instruments) demonstration at school; or the singing of 'Crown Him with Many Crowns' – Eddie had adapted it in the parody, 'Fine Him with Many Fines', for the St John's cricket team; or by the chance discovery of a note in his own hand – 'Hi Mum, give me a nudge at 9.45 am ish, please. Lots of love, Ed x. Actually, have just remembered canvassing at 10am! Best make wake up call at 9.20 ...'

We are blessed in having been sustained through our grieving by the support we have received – and are still receiving – from a wonderful family and many friends, whose acts of kindness have been overwhelming; and, ultimately, through our firm belief that Eddie is now utterly safe in God's keeping and that one day we will be reunited with him.

Clare, Michael, Sarah and their families put their lives on hold for over two weeks leading up to the funeral and burial. We have seen them regularly and been in almost daily communication with them since then. We have also managed to take family holidays together, all 11 of us spending the August bank holiday week in 2006 together in Cornwall, as usual – or almost as usual for this was the first holiday in 24 years without Eddie. It was not and could not have been the same. We missed his huge lounging presence, his sense of fun, his beaming smile and quizzical looks, his slip fielding in beach cricket and his kamikaze runs into the sea, but we mourned his loss and toasted his memory together. The toast was repeated when the family again came together on holiday in Cornwall in 2007, and will be reprised on all like subsequent occasions. This time, however, there were two new additions to our gathering; next year there will be one more. One phase of our family history is over but a new one has begun.

And then there have been the other family events and festivals to celebrate and negotiate. Samuel's baptism was on 1 October 2006. Ed should have been there as God-father. Michael and Frances did not replace him with someone else, but his presence was felt and symbolised in the form of a beautiful butterfly that fluttered between the church wall and the christening party, from time to time settling on the shoulder of Ed's jacket, now worn by Michael.

The Butterfly

Was it a messenger quietly sent on that day?
Could God feel our pain that Ed wasn't there
To cuddle his Godson and add his prayer
As we brought young Samuel into God's care
on that day.

With delicate wings it fluttered about, on that day.
From the wall to Mike's shoulder and back to the wall
It uttered no sound, but was it a call
From heaven to comfort the family all
on that day.

'Be not downcast,' it seemed to say, on that day.
'I'm both with you here, *and* with your son Ed.

With me in heaven, your Eddie's not dead!'
That is, I think, what the butterfly said,
on that day.
(1 October 2006)

Ed was also remembered by his elder brother in a moving tribute at the reception, as he was a few months later by Clare following Katy's baptism, and yet again at the christening of his nephew Reuben Edward in March 2008. The practice of baking cakes for Ed's birthday on 26 October, too, has not yet stopped, what would have been his 25th birthday in 2006 being marked by the production of a round one with a large hole cut out of it to show the hole left in our lives by Ed's death. Sarah said that it looked like a halo. On his birthday, in successive years, we have also all gathered as a family in the cathedral and lit 25 and 26 candles respectively in his memory.

Christmases without Ed have posed further trials. The Christmas service in 2006 left us a helpless, sobbing pair, and at home not even Reuben's birth on Boxing Day could fill the void in our lives. Everyone felt it and we all felt for each other. At Christmas 2007, the pain was less searing, the grief less intense, and although Ed was still acutely missed, we found ourselves making the same family jokes together as we had always done in his life.

Christmas sans Ed

Christmas sans Ed was a strange celebration ...
Tinsel on pictures, lights on the tree,
Presents wrapped brightly for you and for me.
Food all prepared for an army to stay,
Beds snugly made, drinks on the tray –

Then

The troops all arrived with good cheer and a hug,
Children stormed in and rolled on the rug,

The house now filled up with chaos and noise
The floor was quite covered with babies and toys.

Before you knew it

Christmas Day dawned, to Cathedral we dashed,
And into the transept we clattered and crashed
With pushchairs and pram, a nod and a smile
To this one and that as we squeezed down the aisle.

Then

The organ struck up, with choir boys singing
Carols familiar, glad tidings bringing
Of God's only son who lowly was born
To bring light and love to a world so forlorn.

And at that

The tears cascaded, no chance of disguise,
They spurted and poured and flowed from my eyes,
For our deeply loved Ed who'd brought us such light
Had died in Beirut. It didn't seem right.

Yet

At the end of the service, back home we ran,
And checked on the turkey, put veg in the pan
The pudding was heated, the candles were lit
In the blink of an eye round the table we sit.

So

We thanked God for the food with familiar grace,
Then passing and pouring all went on apace
Much chatter, much munching and supping of wine
The tears all forgotten and everything's fine ...

And yet

We kept on discussing what Ed would have said,
And how late he would leave it to get out of bed,
How much he loved pudding with lashings of cream,
How slowly he dried up, he seemed in a dream.

Then

We opened our presents, all given with love,
And played with the little ones sent from above
To comfort our sorrow, give hope to our heart
And know that Ed's death is just life set apart.

But

Familiar presents once more caught me out,
'I must go and see Eddie.' I said with a shout.
Sarah came with me, we jumped in her car
And took to his grave-side a big golden star.

Yes

Christmas sans Ed was a strange celebration
With sadness yet joy, with gloom yet elation.
What was God doing when he made life like this?
The hymn's got it right – all mystery 'tis!

PS

The story's not ended, a postscript I write,
To explain the event which began Christmas night
And later on Boxing Day brought us such joy;
Our Sarah gave birth to her second – a boy!

(Christmas, 2006)

Our friends' willingness to share in the grief of our loss has been of immense importance in our convalescence. As a nineteenth century rabbi once observed, 'Human beings are God's language'; and in the past months many people have responded to a call to be with us – listening to the story of Ed's death, offering us practical support (and, not least, food in the early days), sharing happy memories, hugging us ('no words') and holding our hands, praying for and with us when we found prayer impossible, giving us words of encouragement and extending hospitality.

Many more have given us comfort and reassurance with the written word. Although we must have written and sent scores of condolence letters and cards over the years, as well as receiving them on the deaths of our parents and other loved ones, we never quite realised their importance to bereaved folk until after Eddie's death. Such messages – from casual acquaintances, pupils and former pupils, Ed's student friends, politicians and unknown members of the public, as well as from our own relatives, friends and the church family – are now crammed into four large box files. We were still receiving them some six months after Ed's death, one of the last being a card from the Sikh Gurdwara in Cardiff. And even now Ed is still being remembered by some friends on Christmas cards. 'To Howard and Heather and all your family, both seen and unseen,' writes one; 'I hope that Christmas will be joyous this year, even with Ed's apparent absence', writes another.

Although we knew how widely Ed was loved, as I reread some of those original condolences, I am struck not only by the numbers who wished to share our grief but also by the power of their messages. Many paid their own particular tribute to Ed by recalling their special memories of him. Such comments as 'our sofas never fit[ted] him and we never had enough food and tea!'; and 'he buttered twelve slices of bread' for a picnic with his girlfriend, were as important as those that acknowledged his love, friendship and talents. The amusing reflections, like those 'Eddie T top moments', recounted by his fellow 1st XV second row and 1st XI cricketing friend – 'I'll take a break there', Ed had said after an over of his bowling had cost the team 24 runs, 'no point in making it too close!' – gave particular solace. Similarly comforting – and prophetic – were those who pointed to the strength of our close family and the support of our friends, which they anticipated 'bodes well for your coming to terms with what has happened, for preserving Ed's presence in your hearts and for moving on'. Other friends thought that time would lessen the pain, that Ed's 'spirit, generosity and laughter will never fade' and that our memories of happy times together 'will remain a treasured part of the future too'. And many people gently re-affirmed that Ed was now in the best of places and that we could take comfort from the message of Easter and draw on the strength which God provides. One dear friend urged us to read John Donne's wonderful prayer: 'Bring us, O Lord God, at our last awakening into the house and gate of heaven, to enter into that gate and dwell in that house, where there shall be no darkness nor dazzling, but one equal light; no noise nor silence but one equal music; no fears nor hopes, but one equal possession; no ends nor beginnings, but one equal eternity; in the habitations of thy glory and dominion, world without end'. It remains on my desk and has been committed to memory.

Darkness and Light

Darkness never totally overcame the light.
There were certainly days, weeks, months that felt more
like night –
There are still, and that may always be so.
Yet the darkness never totally overcame the light.

Light came from others, yet sent from above.
Light is assurance and infinite love.
Light is in kindnesses, light's in a touch,
Light is in sympathy, light's in a hug,
Light is in people's prayers, faithfully said,
Light is in messages, 'So sorry he's dead.'

Light is in family, united in grief,
Light is in tears we shed, bringing relief.
Light is the hope we share, light is our joy,
Light is in memories of our precious boy.
Light is in laughter, light's in a look,
Light is in thankfulness and writing this book.

For darkness never really overcame the light.
There were certainly days, weeks, months that felt more
like night –
There are still, and that may always be so.
Yet darkness can never totally overcome the light,
For light is God's love, light is God's power,
Comforting, holding us, hour by hour.

(14 February 2008)

Chapter 9

A Faith Challenged

As for me and my house, we will serve the Lord.
Joshua 24:15
It would be good – not least for my soul – to try and explain
how Ed's death has both affected and been affected by our
ultimate, if sometimes shaky belief in God. I need to begin,
however, with a brief outline of why God enters into this
story at all.

My own faith in the Lord Jesus Christ came to life on
1 February 1981. It is a date that is engraved on my heart.
From that date I changed from being a thoroughly sincere
church-goer, baptized and confirmed in the Church of
England, to a Christian, 'a real one' as I explained to my
close friend, Elizabeth, who had prayed for that very thing
to happen to me. Howard's journey, more of an Emmaus
route than my Damascus Road approach, came to fruition
about two years later. We became bible-reading, grace-
before-meals-saying, house-group attending members of a
lively church near our then home in Crowthorne.

Because of my new-found awareness of God's goodness, I
determined to give our children every opportunity to learn
about Christ for themselves. Weekly Sunday school and
church-going were augmented by regular bible reading and
attendance at Christian holiday camps and in the fullness of
time each one, Eddie included, embraced the Christian faith
and made it their own.

The sense of the love and protection of a Father God, who cares for his children as a good shepherd cares for his sheep, has always been very real to me. I had had a wonderfully strong and protective father myself and so this picture of God was an easy one for me to relate to. Accordingly Howard and I prayed every day for our family to be in God's sure hands. Ed's time in Lebanon was no exception. We certainly had reservations about his choice of destination and I had tried to point out to him some of its drawbacks from the point of view of an anxious mother, but to no avail. So we prayed.

I truly hope that my faith in the triune God is sufficiently mature for me not to be taken in by the slot-machine image: pop in the prayer and out will come the appropriate answer, with change if required. Indeed I have known a number of sincere, loving, prayerful Christians whose lives utterly disprove this theory and who have had to contend with every difficulty known to mankind. Yet I prayed for protection and safety for Ed, trusting that my prayers would be answered. They were not, at least, not in the sense I had intended. Eddie died in Beirut.

Where had God been? Why had he not watched over Ed and kept him safe? So much for faith! So much for prayer! So much for a loving Father God! Where does such a devastating event leave the earnest seeker after God? Definitely confused!

God was, in fact, swiftly on the scene supporting, helping and comforting us, firstly through the touching care and concern of the Embassy staff who looked after us in Beirut. They could not have done more for us. And very importantly, as I lay in that Beirut hotel bed, my heart shrieking out its disbelief that Eddie could have died, God's voice broke through to me in the words of the modern hymn Howard has alluded to elsewhere, 'I am the bread of life'. The words of its chorus kept ringing through my head, 'I will raise him up ...' Even in my shocked, stunned, demented state, I took that as a promise given to me by God. He will raise Eddie up as he raised his own son.

From that moment I made up my mind that none of us, not one single member of the family would lose his or her faith in God. We had lost our beloved Eddie; we were not going to lose God too. What a horridly satisfying victory that would be for the source of all evil! No way would that happen. And in that ghastly night, the most utterly miserable and desolate of our whole lives I turned towards and not away from God. It was a defining moment, but not the end of the story.

That our faith was severely shaken is undeniable. And immediately I am conscious of the difficulty of speaking on behalf of five members of our closely-knit family – and that's not to mention our delightful and supportive in-laws – for each of whom the path has been slightly different. It would therefore be easier to speak of my own journey and give references to the others as and when appropriate.

We returned from Beirut to Hereford on the Saturday. Our son Michael with his wife Frances and baby Samuel had already arrived and shopped for food and prepared for our home-coming, leaving Sarah and family to meet us at Heathrow and drive us home. Clare joined us later on the Sunday, driving down immediately on her return from her holiday in Spain. The home-coming was desperately sad. Eddie was hugely affectionate and deeply loved by every one of us. We struggled to cope with our own grief while seeking to support each other. I just said very firmly, 'None of us is going to lose our faith over this.' I did not realize what a challenge that was going to be for me!

It was probably sheer force of habit which took us to the 8am service in the Cathedral next day, Palm Sunday, but we all felt that was where we wanted to be. We scuttled into the choir stalls just before the procession of clergy came in and tried to open ourselves to receive God's comfort and reassurance. It was very touching that many people thought that the empty seat in our midst was left for Eddie: it was in fact where Samuel's car seat rested with him asleep in it. Needless to say we cried buckets of tears throughout the service and kind friends greeted and hugged us afterwards, also weeping with and for us. As usual, God dispensed his comfort and reassurance through his people.

The following week was a nightmare as we desperately wanted Eddie's body home, but everything seemed set against it – religious holidays, sickening bureaucracy and mistakes in the dating of Ed's death certificate combined to cause delay after delay. One day, it was possibly the Tuesday, while the Dean and Precentor were talking with Howard and rashly assuring us that we could order Ed's funeral just as we liked, I received another phone call from Beirut explaining a further set-back. I rushed distraught into their meeting and screamed hysterically at them, 'Fine sort of God this is! He's supposed to be the creator of the universe yet he can't even get Ed's body back from Beirut!' It was clearly going to be a long road back to anything approaching the childlike trust I'd previously had in God.

I lost my ability to pray and my desire to read the bible. God was several billion miles away and did not look likely to renew contact. Fortunately members of the church did not cease praying and Ed's body was brought back on Easter Saturday, much sooner than had been predicted. One hurdle was over but I continued to feel far distant from God for many, many months after that.

Having the family with us for over two weeks following Ed's death was probably the greatest blessing God bestowed upon us at that time. They were wonderful. They took over the practicalities of life. I found myself incapable of doing anything at all. I could not even dish up a pan of potatoes peeled, chopped and cooked by one of the family. I remember standing holding the pan in one hand, a serving spoon in the other, gazing helplessly at the plates laid out before me, and just not being able to co-ordinate this simplest of operations. It was a dreadful shock to me to see just how paralysed parts of me had become. I was also prone to spells of utter screaming hysteria, as time and again the full enormity and finality of Ed's death swept over me afresh. The loving and accepting arms of a family member were always available to hold and hug me to a calmer state once more.

But it was not all helplessness and hysterics. As Michael noted in his address at Ed's funeral, together we were happy, sad, argumentative and grumpy in turn. We had the three grandchildren to care for and cuddle; we went on long family walks; we watched videos. It was during one of our family walks in the meadows near our house that Sarah announced that there was another little one on the way. The promise of new life. Alleluya!

Besides, there were the important details of Ed's funeral to arrange and for this we called regular family conferences. We would all sit round the dining-room table and give our suggestions and views and, amazingly, everything fell into place with unanimous agreement on every detail. This in itself is something of a miracle, given that we are a family of strong-minded and forthright individuals. God clearly had given us an unusual spirit of consensus. We needed to ensure that our individual addresses would present different facets of our Ed's life and personality. We did not want simply to repeat one another. Again, astonishingly, everything we wanted to say dovetailed to perfection. On the day itself we received the strength to deliver our words and we know that we gave Ed the best send-off we possibly could.

There were the tears and sorrow you would expect at the funeral of a warm, gifted and much-loved young man of twenty-four. But that is not the abiding memory of the service for periodically the Cathedral rang with laughter as one or other of us recounted a clearly appreciated gem from Ed's rich and varied life of wild optimism, missed trains, lost wallets, late arrivals, abandoned cars – all easily recognised foibles of this talented but disorganised son of ours. Then there was the music, each item so carefully chosen to reflect some aspect of Ed's life, all uplifting, moving, rousing; all sung with vigour and passion; all proclaiming our faith in the living God.

Ed's funeral, that celebration of his life, did us a great service; it publicly affirmed that we, the whole family, still believed in a loving God, into whose eternal hands we entrusted our Eddie. At the bleak times that were to follow,

I was so glad of that act of Christian witness. However fragile my faith might become in the future, on that day, 22 April 2006, it was very real. We had asked the vergers to record the service, which they kindly did, and I often play the recording when I am home alone. Although sometimes it leaves me in tears, it never ceases also to lift my heart.

As Howard has explained, the burial the following Monday was a small family affair, and it was desperately hard to see Ed's coffin lowered into the ground. Could this really be the end of our Ed? The words chosen by Andrew Law were wonderfully appropriate, but nothing could diminish the deep sense of loss, the leaden sadness which then took hold of our hearts. With no more preparations or arrangements to be made there was just a massive hole in our lives where Eddie should have been. The rest of our family went back to their own homes to resume the lives they had put on hold to be with us. It was too hard to go back to our empty house. We went to Mellor and stayed in the home of kind friends for the rest of the week. Where was God now? How would our faith help?

During this time my strongest urge was to rant and rail at God for his disservice to us and to the world by his premature calling of Eddie to heaven. Why Eddie? Ed was such a lovely person. Ed was on God's side! He was one of the good influences in the world. He generated love and smiles. Why kill him off when there are child-molesters and sadistic murderers and the like who are doing the world no good at all? Not, as I hastened to add to anyone who was listening to my ranting, that I wanted anyone else dead instead, but just that I could not see any divine purpose being accomplished by Ed's untimely death.

Howard and I walked out in the hills and the strenuous exercise and closeness to nature did a little to soothe – or at least physically exhaust us. The great frustration I experienced was that I couldn't scream at God as I longed to do; although there were not many people about, there were always a few just in hearing range. I did not want some happy hiker to imagine that Howard was attacking me.

Now, fifteen months on, I would still like to howl out my lament to God, but the intensity of that desire has subsided a little, just as I no longer feel quite so intensely the urge to smash windows – an urge my innate carefulness with money has kept in check!

The other deeply felt desire was to cut open my stomach and let out some of the pain. The grief and anguish I experienced at Ed's death was an intense physical pain. I was sure that a clinical injury causing such pain would have given me a heart attack and killed me off. I could not believe that I could be experiencing such agony and still live. At times it became almost too much and I did not know where to turn to keep on going. I felt that opening up my stomach with a nice sharp, rounded knife would let out some of the anguish. I could even picture it as a disgusting greeny-yellow gunk which would gush out of the wound. For the first time I felt I had found some understanding of why people under great stress harm themselves.

Throughout this period I continued to feel that God was a far distant entity, not remotely interested in me or my grief. I would beg him to reduce the agony and distress and reach the point of turning my back on him altogether. He was totally useless! Nothing altered. Then either the phone would ring with our daughter, Sarah, calling for a chat; or a friend would knock tentatively at the door. God might well have been keeping his own distance, but he made sure his servants kept in touch. Indeed our children worked out something akin to a rota of care for us. It was hard being at home with Eddie memories all round us, but some member of the family would contrive to be there with us as we returned from our frequent trips away, and in between times, we spent much of our time at one of their homes. Being surrounded by our family did not reduce the heartache, but it adjusted our focus.

Night-time was a real trial for me. It was a long, long time before I slept through a night once more, and I spent many hours awake and sobbing into my pillow. I was also beset with horrid dreams and even worse thoughts which made

me fearful of night-time. As and when I did manage at least
to doze at least for a while, I would wake up with the sickening knowledge of Ed's death sweeping afresh into my
consciousness. It was like hearing the news in Beirut all over
again.

Here is where email came to be such a boon for me. I did
not like to wake Howard who was just escaping from our
crushing sadness for a few precious, peaceful hours, and,
although friends generously assured me I could ring them
day or night, I really did not think it a reasonable thing to
do! But I could send an SOS email, knowing that I wasn't
waking the chosen recipient, but at least I was able to
express something of the anguish and cry out for help
knowing that they would read it and respond in due course
– invariably very promptly. My cries for help were on two
fronts, but closely related: how could I cope with my grief;
and where on earth was God in all this?

The most pestered email correspondents, though by no
means the only ones, come from different wings of the
Christian church. One was a Jesuit priest, Fr Nick King,
who had been Ed's 'spiritual adviser' in Oxford, and the
other was Paul Towner, the vicar from our local evangelical
church. Val Hamer from the Cathedral held the middle
ground – in churchmanship, I mean. I should add that they
also gave us their time face to face. That I did not lose either
my sanity, or ultimately my faith, was in no small part due
to their understanding, prayers, unfailing support, and their
deep wells of wisdom. In preparing to write this chapter I
printed off our correspondence and was deeply shocked and
embarrassed to see how much I had dumped on them, not
just at night, but at all times of the day. My doubts, my
fears, my grief, my anger were poured out, often amidst
streams of tears. The process of expressing my feelings
brought me some sense of peace, and their calm reassurance
would later reinforce it. Could I really doubt that a loving
God was at work? Yes, my heart protested. Surely a loving
God would not have let Ed die.

With hindsight, I can see that God never ceased to hold us

in his heart. That was not so clear to me in the yawning depths of my grieving, where all I could feel was pain and all I could see was a sad, bleak future ahead. I remember making a superhuman effort to comfort Clare, saying that yes, we are distressed beyond words now, but we would resurface. Failing to do so would display such a lack of gratitude for all the other good things we have been blessed with. Anyway, Ed would hate it if we let his death damage our appreciation of all that we still have. I think I was talking myself into it as much as Clare, but a tiny bit of me did believe it. Paul had also told us about other people, who had lost children, but had in time picked up the threads of their lives once more and lived positively. I hoped this could be true for us.

It is perhaps worth adding here that one persistent and unhelpful notion we had to fight off was that any let-up in our grief would be a betrayal of Ed. It would mean that we were leaving him behind. Clare, Sarah and I talked of this frequently over the year or so following Ed's death. We none of us wanted to think that he would slip from our minds, from our lives. I am utterly certain this will never happen and indeed, Clare, Michael and Sarah talk to their own children about 'Uncle Eddie'. None of the little ones can possibly remember Eddie as they were all so young – or not even born – when he went to Beirut, but they can pick him out in family photos and we talk about him to them as naturally as we talk about the rest of the family. So far none of them has asked where Eddie is. It will be interesting to see how this question is handled in due course.

It was in response to this deep anxiety that I wrote my 'Dialogue' with Eddie, where he gently assured me that we were not leaving him behind but coming towards him. That reassuring perspective cheered me immensely.

A dialogue with Eddie

'I took some flowers up to your grave today, Ed.'

'That's nice, Mum.'

'I wanted to bring you home with me, Ed.'

'I am home, Mum.'

'You know what I mean, Eddie Boy!'

'I know what you mean, Mum. Sorry.'

'I don't like leaving you, darling.'

'You haven't left me, Mum.
You cannot ever leave me.
I'm always with you.
I'm in your heart.
I live each day with you.
Wherever you go, I go.
You will not leave me, Mum.'

'I don't want to leave you, Ed.'

'I know, Mum. Ssh, now. Don't cry.
Look at it this way, Mum.
I'm not behind you, I'm ahead!
You're not leaving me behind;
You're coming towards me.'

'That's nice, Ed. I love you, darling.'

'I love you, too, Mum.'

(6 May 2007)

Chapter 10

Hanging on to God

Many people said to us how lucky we were to have our faith. What a blessing it must be for us. Even in my most mean-spirited moments I would probably agree that a battered faith is better than no faith, but Ed's death threw up more questions and doubts than reassuring certainties. It was going to take some serious readjusting.

What has become clear to me in writing this is that challenged though my faith was by Ed's pointless and unnecessary death, at no stage did I actually doubt the existence of God. I was angry with him, resentful of the fact he had allowed this tragedy to happen; and I certainly would not trust him any further than I could proverbially throw him, but I still believed he was there. The real issue I faced was trying to rebuild my relationship with him, something that a very large part of me simply did not want to do. I did not feel I could love him and I did not much like the way he behaved!

Making things worse was the crushing burden of guilt I felt at this. Fine specimen of a Christian I am! I can love God while things are going along OK with just the normal ups and downs of life, but face me with one tragedy and I back off with just a simmering resentment left to show for my so-called faith! Not a pretty picture to live with. I was also acutely aware of other people facing similar and infinitely greater tragedies. Why should we have a smoother run than anyone else? I shouldn't be asking, Why us? Why Ed? Equally valid questions are, Why not us? Why not Ed? Bad things happen in this imperfect world. We see them daily on our TV screens and read about them in the papers. We know personally of many others who have lost children through illness or road accidents or other disasters.

Our elder daughter, Clare, summed it up to perfection. She said that she could see on the news whole villages in Africa being wiped out by war or AIDS and still affirm that there is a loving God. But having our Eddie die was a different matter altogether! She deliberately expressed it starkly to make her point, but it was one to which we could all accede. It was most certainly my position. Yet we clung on.

Clare said that she wasn't sure what she believed for herself any more, but she still wanted her two year old son Oliver and as yet unborn daughter to go to a church where there was a good children's ministry so that they could learn about Christ. Sarah expressed her anxiety about praying for her little daughter, Esther. We had all faithfully prayed for Ed and see what happened. Perhaps it's best not to draw attention to ourselves. Yet she and her family continued attending their church where she gained great comfort and renewed strength. Michael spoke at his son's christening on 1 October that year. Eddie should have been one of Samuel's Godfathers. Michael said that we might question why Eddie had to die so young, and we'll not know the answer this side of heaven. But he knew from his reading of the bible that we live in a fallen world where sad and bad things happen. He and his wife Frances still wanted Samuel to be baptized, to be brought up in the faith of Christ, just as Ed had been. Each in our own way, we all clung on. We were just not sure what we were clinging to.

Interestingly, although our personal prayer-life and bible reading took a long sabbatical, Howard and I did not stop attending church. I am not sure why this was. Even now, more than two years after Ed's death, we occasionally shed at least a few tears during services. In the early days I sobbed almost uncontrollably for long stretches of time. The words of a hymn or the bible reading would either have an Eddie association, or else would strike me as blatantly untrue in the light of Ed's death. A favourite hymn of mine based on Psalm 121 is called 'I lift my eyes to the quiet hills' – we chose this setting for the psalm at Ed's funeral. Yet singing it at an evening service in St Peter's church some months later reduced me to pulp. Verse three ends, 'My shepherd will guard his sheep,' and verse four, 'the Lord will preserve his own.' My indignant heart shrilled out, 'Does he indeed? Well, where was he when Ed died? Not much guarding and preserving that night, was there?' It does not take countless similar examples to illustrate my state of mind.

Nevertheless we continued to attend the Cathedral every Sunday morning and the parish churches of St. Peter's and St James' in the evenings. They were both beautiful and difficult in different ways. The Cathedral has so many associations with Eddie as it is the church we have attended as a family every Sunday morning since September 1987. I could see Eddie everywhere: a little lad taking part in Christmas crib services; a server carrying the cross or candle; a young adult beaming a welcome for me as I came in from Sunday school; an usher at his sisters' weddings. In a sense these pictures were lovely, but any comfort derived from them was countered by the awful knowledge that the last time he was there he lay in his coffin. I would never see him there alive again. I longed to feel God's comfort. I prayed each week that I would hear his voice. But all I heard were my own distraught thoughts. These were in no way uplifting or reassuring, just downright distressing. I really wondered why I kept going at all. I could have had those thoughts at home.

Amidst the small, intimate evening congregation of St Peter's and St James' parish churches – somewhere between one and two dozen people attend – I found it easier to accept offered love and compassion and receive them as a gift from God. But I also felt very exposed and vulnerable as there was definitely no hiding place when my emotions got the better of me – no big pillars behind which I could hide my flowing tears. I did not like the idea that I was embarrassing or upsetting other worshippers.

Nevertheless, every member of the family would affirm their conviction that we have been deeply blessed by the Christian family everywhere embracing and upholding us. We have had our own congregations loving and praying for us. We have had churches all over the world saying prayers and offering masses for Ed. People we have not known prayed because they knew Ed, and people who had never known Eddie prayed because they knew us. At a time when we ourselves could not utter a single word of prayer, we were grateful and touched to know that others held us up to the loving Lord Jesus and asked him to bless and comfort us.

It is difficult to explain what this blessing and comfort meant in practice. Howard and I were frequently devastated by our sense of helplessness in the face of Ed's death. All those years of careful watching over, protecting and nurturing our little lad had come to naught. Out in Beirut, in a hostel with a faulty shower heater, he had died and we had been able to do nothing to save him. Coupled with this helplessness was the nagging uncertainty, were we in any way to blame for his death? Could we have prevented it? The simple answer to these questions is no, and this recurring cycle of 'if only this or that' is not just pointless but positively destructive, as our rational side increasingly allows us to recognize. It is just incredibly difficult to engage a rational side when crushed with grief. This is where the SOS emails and their replies came so much into their own. These offered not just moral support and good sense – though these in themselves were greatly valued – but also a God-given wisdom, usually dispensed with a large portion of humour which is an essential ingredient in my life.

Take, for example, the night-time torments that I was in some way responsible for Ed's death. After all, to my distraught mind, if we had not planned to visit Ed in Beirut, he would not have been looking for somewhere for us to stay and discovered in the 'Lonely Planet Guide' the *pension* where he had died. I firmly believed that this irrational fear would rob me of my sanity. Nick King clearly pointed out whence such thoughts came; told me to have no truck with them; and assured me that they would flee if I stood up to them. He suggested I should turn round to face them and say 'boo' to them, and they would run away. The 'boo' made me smile and the thought of actually saying it in the middle of the night made me laugh out loud. He added, 'Try putting a large sign up inside your head that says, "No entry for unwanted voices"'. I went to bed that night rehearsing my lines, and that in itself proved enough. I was not awakened by them again. The same thoughts still occasionally try to creep into my head but their power to distress and torture has been destroyed.

Rather than continuing with a random list of examples of this nature, I shall try to identify some of the areas which are beginning to help me in my on-going attempts to rebuild my faith in God. I must emphasise that it is still very much a 'work in progress' and I continue to experience a reluctance to give myself whole-heartedly to God once more. Something just below my rib-cage holds back. A caution, a reserve remains. But I am now confident that it is within God's power to draw me closer and that he will do so – in good time. This is one hugely important area where all my email correspondents have been so supremely helpful: they have never rushed me nor have they ever made me feel guilty about my feelings. They have always treated them with the utmost respect. For this I am deeply grateful.

In quietness and trust is your strength. Isaiah 30:15
To rebuild my relationship with God, I needed to tackle the area of trust. How could I ever trust him again? This is closely related to what on earth is prayer all about and how could I persuade myself to even try praying after what had happened to much prayed for Ed. Then the question arises, am I capable of loving God once more? Also, as a good bible-reading Christian positioned somewhere towards the

evangelical wing, I was accustomed to reading the bible daily. I knew that this, too, was important to rebuild my faith, but I simply did not feel like doing it. A further area that was and still is important for the whole family is trying to get some grip on the notion of eternal life, linked with 'What is heaven like?' We want to know for absolutely certain sure that we shall be with Ed again and that we shall know him. The problem with faith in general and mine particularly in my present state is that it is almost by definition lacking in absolute certainty. Overarching and linking all these issues stands the central question: what is the nature of this God I insist on clinging to? Who or what am I seeking to trust, love and pray to, and finally join in heaven at the end of my days? What, indeed, is God like?

In his commentary on Romans chapter 9, Nick King talks of God's sovereign freedom to do exactly as he pleases, 'Like a 400lb gorilla.' Help! Similarly, Paul Towner preached a sermon on God's sovereignty, with the sub-title 'Scary God'. Could I love and trust a God who has the almighty and sovereign power to act like a scary 400lb gorilla? It is a challenge, but very reluctantly I have to admit that there is little choice. Howard and I were helpless to prevent Eddie's death. Life seems to hang on a thread as fine as a spider spins. I have no control over it. That leaves me with either nothing at all to hold onto, or the scary sovereign God.

This has probably been one of the hardest hurdles for me to get over. God was the only one who could have prevented Ed's pointless and unnecessary death in his Beirut hostel. He, in his sovereign and almighty power chose not to. Why is that? We feel badly let down. Like Job, I question God and ask him, 'Why Ed? Why did he let Ed die?' Then I fancy a chill come over me as I hear God's words from the closing chapters of the Book of Job, 'Who is this that darkens my counsel with words without knowledge? Will the one who contends with the Almighty correct him?' I do not know how to respond. I am quiet in the presence of the Almighty. It is not a comfortable silence. But I have to ask, 'Is this the God I have to trust, the God who seems to act so randomly?' I can sing choruses about trusting God only with a degree of reserve, or at best, a wry smile.

One suggestion which helped was to think in terms of a marriage where trust has been destroyed by infidelity. Clearly rebuilding that trust will take time. It cannot be rushed. Slowly the wound will heal. I can certainly now entrust my family, friends and their situations to God in prayer without thinking that this is asking for trouble, but the scar remains. Perhaps it always will remain this side of heaven.

The other side of the coin from the all powerful God is the seemingly vulnerable and ineffective God. As I cannot accept that God is actually the source or author of evil, I wonder why he in his almighty power does not overcome it. Is he actually able to? In one perplexed email after another I grappled with this. Is God just like the last fairy Godmother in the children's story, who cannot undo the spell of the wicked fairy that condemns the princess to prick her finger on a spinning wheel and die? All she can say is that after 100 years, a handsome prince will come and bring Sleeping Beauty back to life with a kiss. Is this what God is like? Is he helpless in the face of the enemy who wreaks havoc on the world? Can he only mop up our tears afterwards and try to make things better for us?

I will be the first to agree that we have indeed been the recipients of God's compassion and love generously, even lavishly expressed through others, and that many good things have come out of Ed's death. But I will scream from the house-tops that in my considered opinion that has certainly not made Ed's death acceptable or in any way 'worth it'. No way! Not at all! Not one tiny little bit! And yet I return time and again to this position: do I accept and trust this almighty yet vulnerable, even ineffectual, God? I answer with the words of Peter. 'Where else can I turn? You, Lord, have the words of eternal life.' Without God, life is purposeless and pointless and I cannot believe that.

To complement these two apparently contradictory pictures of God, there is the God of love, who both loves us and expects

our love in return. Interestingly, rediscovering my love for God
has not been so difficult a task as rebuilding my trust. By
early July 2006, I was able to say in my house-group that I
wanted to **want** to love God again, and then, in stages over the
coming months I felt that love surge up once more from within the depths of my heart. Then one day during a church service the following January, the words of the general confession
came up in neon lights: I have not loved God with my whole
heart. Have I ever? I wondered. But now it seemed important
to try and address the issue. Only I cannot in my own
strength. Without God's unlimited grace I am powerless to move
forward. The best I can do is acknowledge the love God has
poured out on me and my family and respond to that love as
any human does, by loving in return. I do not love the fact that
God let Ed die and again, I am not sure that I shall ever be able
to eradicate that resentful thought. But I am prepared to leave
it in God's hands and to his perfect timing to move into even
those deep recesses of my heart.

I am thankful for the prayers which have enabled me,
enabled all the family, to take the steps we have towards
coping with our grief and rebuilding our relationship with
God. I wish they had been my prayers. But as I explained
earlier, our prayer-life vanished without trace when Ed died.
Our habit of well over twenty years, of beginning each day
by reading some verses of the bible together, then praying
for the day ahead fell into disuse. There seemed no point.
Interestingly enough, I was happy to ask others to pray for
us and for our family. I recognized how vulnerable we all
were to spiritual attack and I desperately wanted us all to be
protected. I couldn't bring myself to pray so I asked others
to pray for us. It was a great relief and comfort to know that
we were being sustained by the prayers of faithful others
while our own faith was at rock-bottom. This is illogical,
but logic does not come into coping with grief.

It was a great breakthrough when on 27 July 2006 we
made an enormous effort, gritted our teeth, (not very
gracious!) and gave it our all. For the first time since Ed had
died I managed to tell God, in the midst of much sobbing,

just how hard every member of the family had found Ed's death; the issues and questions and grief we were all struggling with; and how each one of us needed his grace to come through ultimately strengthened, not weakened in our faith. This prayer produced a significant crack in the barrier which I, in my grief, had erected between me and God.

I still wonder what prayer is all about, but I pray. I have better conversations with God while I am thinking or writing than I do when I am consciously praying. My questions are not answered, I still long to understand, but instead I receive a temporary peace or a calm which, for a little while, satisfies my soul.

As for bible reading, another tool I needed to mend my damaged relationship with God, that was made easier by the present Nick King gave us at a memorial cricket match for Eddie played at the St John's cricket ground on 27 May. It was a copy of the New Testament which Nick himself had translated and interspersed with his commentary and study guide. It makes great reading. As it says on the cover, it is 'freshly translated' and Nick's choice of word or phrase is frequently surprising, even startling. Often what Nick wrote made me smile, sometimes I frowned, but I read it. In the end I was able to write to Nick to say to say how much good it was doing me to 'bathe' in God's word.

It was not, as I once famously protested, all 'cosy, cosy comfort', and I argued and debated with the bible as I read it. I still do. I had, for example, greatly mixed feelings on reading of Lazarus being raised from the dead. On one level I was with the crowd who said, 'Could not the one who opened the eyes of the blind man have brought it about that this one should not die?' Yes, I vehemently interjected, could not the one who did all those miracles have kept Ed from dying? And both sisters remonstrated with him that he had not come in time to save Lazarus. Indeed! I thought. Nor Eddie! Then when Lazarus was raised once more I felt cheated. Ed was not raised. And yet – I always find that there is an 'and yet' – my heart cannot help responding with Martha's declaration, 'I have come to believe that you are the Messiah, the Son of God.'

I cannot claim that all is now right between me and God. As I explained earlier, this rebuilding is a work in progress. I have moments when the light penetrates through to my heart, and periods when darkness appears to have the upper hand. I can truly say that we are deeply thankful for the twenty-four and a half years we had with Ed. We have absolutely nothing to regret in that precious time spent with Ed in the midst of our family. Throughout every minute we loved him to bits and he loved us. Yet we are so desperately sad that it was only twenty-four and a half years. Similarly we are immensely and intensely grateful for the love and compassion that has been showered on us as a family since Ed's death, but that gratitude does not dispel the pain of permanent absence from our beloved son and brother. The grief remains.

Similarly I am so grateful to my spiritual advisers who gave me permission to grieve loud and long, and encouraged me to let my heart be heard. It was a great relief as well, to be told that I do not have to reconcile my rational and my emotional sides. Both are valid. They can live alongside each other. Yet however great such wisdom and understanding has been our sadness and desolation remain. It is, Nick said, the price we pay for loving Ed. We would not wish it any other way.

Light moments and dark, thankfulness and grief, appreciation for what still have and sadness at what we have lost, all these live alongside each other. One does not cancel out the other. We are just developing a *modus vivendi,* a way of living with the situation we are powerless to change. This is the acceptance or 'surrender' so often referred to in my emails. It does not come easily to me. I argue and protest too much. Yet I have to admit that a partial trust has been rebuilt and large portions of my heart are open once more to my loving if unpredictable, almighty and sovereign God.

Chapter 11

Heaven and Healing

But our citizenship is in heaven. Philippians 3:20
We had some anxious moments in the early weeks after Ed
died. Was Eddie, now that he's in heaven, missing us as
much as we were missing him? That would be dreadful. We
were deeply grateful to Val Hamer for suggesting (for
indeed she does not know either!) that as Ed is now in eternity and outside the constraints of time, we might already
be with him in heaven while still being without him here on
earth. We liked that idea and accepted it readily, but we do
not really *know*.

Just what is heaven like? What is the eternal life which
our lovely Ed is living now? As Nick King admitted, the
bible is very coy when it tries to talk about it. Yet how I
wish I knew! I feel wrong footed by my inadequacy in trying
to give heaven some shape. I am embarrassed that all my
images are trite, childish, both self-centred and Eddie-
centred. I want to picture a place where Ed is happy and I
focus on the things he enjoyed here with us. I wonder
whether singing God's praises round the Throne of Grace
would seem quite so much fun as hitting magnificent sixes
into neighbouring gardens or tennis courts. Do they indeed,
play cricket at all in heaven? Is Ed listening appreciatively
to familiar tales retold by my father? Is there a nice big
grand piano on which Ed can bash out his favourite tunes?
At least there'll be plenty of company for our gregarious

son. Eddie loved spending time with family and friends.

The poem I wrote on the first Eddie birthday we faced after his death gives clear indications of my groping towards a happy place for Ed to be.

Eddie's Birthday

It's Eddie's birthday. Where is Ed?
Ed's not here, for he is dead.
We gather round and weep and sigh.
Why did Eddie have to die?
Ambitious, gentle, funny, kind,
Large of frame and sharp of mind,
Well known to all for being late,
Yet early at the Pearly Gate?

Was there an urgent heavenly call
For someone who could hit a ball
Right out of the Celestial Ground,
In fact so far, it can't be found?
Perhaps you heard they need a hand
An oboe short in the angelic band,
Or pianist who'll really crash
The tunes out at the eternal bash.

Could God not wait? He needed you
To fill some gap, 'Yes, Ed will do.'
Someone whose knowledge, talent, wit,
Someone whose profile you could fit?
A croquet match? A grand debate?
Rugby fixture? Dinner date?
We just don't know and so we sigh,
Why did Eddie have to die?

You were not perfect, that we know.
We lived with you! My grey hairs show
The worry, stress, indeed frustration
Of lightning dashes to the station

To catch the train, retrieve the phone,
Find your luggage – then speed home
For wallet left, or was it lost?
My shattered nerves would count the cost.

Your grandiose plans, exotic, wild,
Would leave us anxious. Can our child
Pull this one off? Then roof-top walk,
The skylight smashed, insurance talk,
We must consider who will pay
For all the damage done that day.
It's just as well we were not told
Of all your escapades so bold!

We miss you, Ed.
We miss your hugs; we miss your care,
Your hulking self upon the chair,
Your walking with us arm in arm,
Your deep discussion, fun and charm.
We miss your presence, warm and true.
We miss your phone calls, emails, too.
We so much love you, miss you, Ed.
Can it be true that you are dead?

But wait?
Is that a distant voice I hear?
'Your Ed's not dead – he's just up here!'
(26 October 2006)

When the children were small we used to play and sing along to *Kids' Praise* tapes. One song goes something like this, 'Heaven is a wonderful place, filled with glory and grace, I'm wanna see my Saviour's face, Heaven is a wonderful place. (I wanna go there!)' That seemed a suitably attractive if vague picture before Ed died, but now I want some detail please. Another picture designed for children but which once upon a time satisfied my mind is that of the caterpillar and butterfly. Here we are on earth, like caterpillars, happily munching our way along some dark green cabbage leaves, quite unable to picture anything better. But once we move through the chrysalis stage, death, we become beautiful butterflies with infinitely more to know and enjoy. Yes, but *what* will we know and enjoy?

I have never wavered in my belief that heaven is a more inviting prospect than hell! Whether in your mind's eye you envisage hell as the eternally burning, sulphuric flames and malicious demons beloved of medieval artists, or the less gruesome but infinitely desolate picture of the total absence of God, heaven is definitely the better option. But I really want to know more.

Recently I turned to the Book of Revelation and skimmed through chapters 19 to 21. My heart fleetingly soared as I grasped and absorbed the magnificent images of glory before my eyes settled on the words, 'God will wipe away every tear from their eyes. And death shall be no more; and sadness, and crying and pain shall be no more – for the former things have gone.' I was caught up in John's vision and my heart surged with joy before tears of repentance poured down my face as I asked God's forgiveness for my ungraciously nagging questions and my lack of understanding. I felt so sorry that my pictures of heaven are trite and simplistic and childish. I wished I had not thought that singing God's praises round the Throne of Grace was not so much fun as playing cricket. I wished I could recapture that brief experience of surging joy. I cannot. It was a gift from God for that moment. It was not for me to hold. Just as at this Easter, 2007, Clare was given a real insight into the meaning of resurrection and a greatly reassuring understanding of Ed in glory. Neither of these glimpses can be retained, examined, dissected. It must be enough that they were.

One thing which can be looked at time and again is a new memorial to St Ethelbert which, as Howard explained in chapter 5, has been recently dedicated in the Cathedral. There is an inscription for Eddie beneath one of the panels. In this context, however, it is not the inscription that is important but the placing of it beneath the picture of poor Ethelbert about to have his head chopped off. At Ethelbert's side there waits an angel, poised to place a martyr's crown on his head. For us, that martyr's crown is Ed's crown of glory, the follow-up to Clare's sense of Ed now in glory. Amen.

One final coda to this section is a comment made in one of Nick's emails, where he drew attention to the fact that we have never doubted that Ed is in heaven. Nor have we. We have no firmer grasp of what heaven is like, but we know Ed is there. One day, we shall join him.

God has torn us and will heal us. Hosea 6:1
This text was used by the Dean of Gloucester in his address given on the occasion of the opening service of the Three Choirs Festival in August 2007. It caused me some problems when I checked it in the bible as the clear inference is that God has deliberately torn us. This is not a comfortable thought and I have to ask, for what purpose? The Dean continued, 'I cannot tell you why God has torn us and solve the mystery of suffering but I do believe he heals us.' It is in some attempt to describe and explain the healing that is taking place in all of us that I continue now.

The image I have of myself when we heard of the news of Ed's death is that of a large mirror, shattered into a thousand pieces. When trying to help me understand the pain and weariness we were still experiencing well over twelve months later, Paul Towner wrote, 'The whole of your inner emotional and relational map has been savagely torn up and thrown away . . .' Yet another picture I have is that of a huge hole in our hearts, in our lives, in our family. Every family photo taken since Ed's died has emphasised the massive absence that his death has created. Shattered, torn up, shot through with a shell hole: how can such damage ever be healed?

In one sense, I fear that it never will be totally healed, but it would be churlish not to acknowledge the healing that has taken place. As has become clear from what I have

already written, the love of our family, our friends and our
churches has been central. Clare has described our life since
Ed died as 'walking through the valley of the shadow of
death'. Having so many compassionate companions on the
way has been a real gift from God.

And our growing brood of grandchildren has brought us
a great bonus of joy – a counter-balance to our sorrow.
They in no way replace Ed, of course, and we are so sad
that they will never know their uncle Eddie, but cuddling
the babies, playing with the older ones, reading stories to
them, seeing them develop, and, above all, experiencing
their utterly unconditional love, that has been balm to our
souls.

Grandchildren apart, for as yet, they are better noise-
makers than listeners, one of the greatest gifts which our
loving companions have given us is a listening ear. I am still
amazed that so many people realized that listening was the
key. We did not want advice. We did not want to hear of
even more tragic stories. We did not want trite truisms:
'time will heal' and the like. We wanted to tell our story and
talk about our Ed. We love talking about Eddie. Our faces
brighten. We have to smile. Smiles bring healing. I thank
God for the listeners.

Howard has written about the hundreds of cards and
letters and flowers we received when Ed died. Reading them
was of course desperately sad, but learning more of Eddie's
escapades from his many good friends, sensing the deep
affection in which he was held, knowing that his all too
short life had been filled with love and laughter did make
things a little better. In the same way, all the memorial
events – from church services to cricket matches, from
Greek drama to debates – have had a similar bitter-sweet
effect, but with sweetness uppermost. Most of these events
have been arranged by his friends. Such generous giving of
their time and talents to remember Ed and celebrate his
many-faceted life is so touching. Once again it warms our
hearts. Eddie's death was unnecessary and pointless, but his
life was not in vain.

Beyond all that family and friends and church have given, there are five things I would like to highlight as important in our healing. They are tears, routine, music, writing and laughter.

Tears are a natural response to grief and are too obvious to need explanation. Suffice it to say that Lake Ontario could probably be refilled with the tears we have shed and continue to weep for our precious Ed. I only want here to declare a deep debt of gratitude to those who have declined to be embarrassed by such an un-English display of emotion and instead have waited patiently for us to recover or have wept with us. Such empathy and understanding have allowed the tears to help in our healing. Repressing them would have hindered our road to recovery.

If tears sound obvious, routine sounds boring, but for us it was hugely beneficial just to get back to the things we do each day. For Howard it meant resuming his roles as school governor and charity trustee; returning to his research and writing; attending conferences as a Bishops' adviser on ordination and chairing the local Historical Association – as well as watching as much cricket as possible, of course! For me, it was going back to the school where I teach and being instantly absorbed into the maelstrom of activity which is term-time in a junior school. The timing for the resumption of these activities needed to be right. It would not have helped us to use frantic activity to sublimate our grief – besides which, we didn't (and still don't) have the energy for frantic activity! We lived in a state of perpetual weariness. For a long time we struggled to get through each day. So it was a matter of gently feeling our way forward and picking up threads as we felt able.

I began this section by referring to the Dean of Gloucester's text; God has torn us and will heal us. He went on to say 'I believe that music can be part of that healing process.' For Howard this has certainly been true. One of the first activities he started again after Ed's death was singing in the Hereford Choral Society and preparing for the 2006 Three Choirs Festival. It has at times been difficult as much music from our great choral tradition is very moving, and music speaks directly to the soul. There are times when he has had to stop singing, if only for a bar, to recover his composure, as in 2006 when singing Elgar's, 'The Kingdom', or the following year, in Hymnus Paradisi, composed by Howell as a memorial for his own son. But hard though it may have been on occasion he would be the first to say how healing music has been for him.

Much as I love singing, especially hymns, I am not a good enough musician to join a choir and my equivalent creative activity has been writing. I write all the time, on train journeys, while waiting for appointments, early in the morning before most people are awake and late into the evening. Mostly I write letters and emails, but I also compose an unsophisticated sort of poetry. Since Ed has died, much of what I have written relates directly or indirectly to him. I have found healing in trying to find the words to express my grief, our grief. It has helped me greatly to cope with things. Once I am able to write about them, the grimmest moments, the most nightmarish thoughts gain a sense of proportion. They lose their irrational, hysterical edge.

Take for example a desperately distressing dream I had in the April, after Ed died and before his funeral. Ed was lying across the back of an estate car, not dead, but clearly close to death. He had a pillow under his feet, but nothing for his head. I gently removed the pillow from the foot end and placed it under his head and held him. I didn't know what he made of dying and all the funeral arrangements going on round him, and I wanted to try and talk to him about it. I asked him 'What do you think about all this Ed?' deliberately keeping it vague – could be the dying or the funeral – so as to upset him as little as possible. He looked at me and said, 'I just don't know Mum.'

I then woke up utterly, screamingly distraught – my little boy had certainly not wanted to die! I could not tell anyone else as the whole family was already grief-stricken beyond words. I couldn't add this uncertainty to their sadness. They all knew I was deeply troubled but wouldn't tell them, and we tried to think who I could talk to. After several false starts, I got in touch with Andrew Law, who gave the address at Ed's funeral, and sobbed my story to him over the phone. He said that he thought my dream was not about Ed not wanting to die, but about my sadness over not being able to hold him at any point. The pillow beneath his feet was there because I had held Ed's feet very briefly at the dreadful apology for a morgue in Beirut.

That calmed me greatly and the dream was not such a big issue again until early March 2007, when it came stabbing back into my recollection and grieved me all over again. I was seeing Val Hamer, the Chancellor at the Cathedral, anyway, so amidst deep sobs, I told her about it, and she said that in my dream, Ed had not been dead, so he was just being honest in saying he wasn't sure. She felt I needed another dream. I was still on this train of thought at church on Sunday evening. I arrived home and desperately wanted to write one of my 'poems', so I did.

The poem needs just one further piece of clarification, and that is to recall the occasion I described in chapter 1 about Ed when he was three and a half years old, and had first heard the Easter story in Sunday school. 'Where's de body?' he asked us, greatly excited by the mystery. Those words became a vital part of the poem.

The Dream

My son lies in the car
My arm supports his neck,
My eyes look in his face,
'What do you think, Ed?'
'I'm just not sure, Mum.'

The words which froze my heart,
The phrase that pierced my soul,
The angst that blew my mind,
'I'm just not sure, Mum.'

The dream I cannot tell
The fear I cannot speak,
The thought I cannot share,
'I'm just not sure, Mum.'

Dear Lord, I need your help
To get me through this phase.
Please send another dream
To say that Ed's now safe.

'The Easter story, Mum,
I learned when I was small,
The "where's de body?" one –
I know the answer, now!'

'Just don't you worry, Mum,
God knows you are not sure.
I wasn't sure myself!
But now I'm very sure.'

(4 March 2007)

I haven't had the second dream, but perhaps God knows that I don't really need it now – although I would certainly still like it. Having written about it, I can look that dream in the eye and not be tortured by it.

I am deeply grateful to those chosen few who have read my demented ramblings at my rawest moments. I am also grateful that God uses this means to enable me to feel my way tentatively towards him – much like the psalmists, who begin with anger or despair but end by praising God for his surpassing greatness. I have not, as yet, gone that far, but I don't rule it out as a future possibility!

The final factor which I want to mention is laughter. It is impossible to overstate how much laughter has helped us all to cope. Laughter does not sound appropriate for those who are mourning but as a family we have always quipped and teased and seen the funny side of things. It comes as naturally to us as breathing. Eddie laughed a lot. He had a brilliant sense of fun. I'm sure he still has. I bet he loves it when we fall about in helpless mirth over one of the children's antics or some comical situation or an idiotic thing one of us has said or done. After a thoroughly good session of utterly helpless, chortling mirth, we always feel so much better. Laughter can, of course, turn rapidly to tears as we wish Ed could be with us to share the moment, but when we join him in heaven the tears will be gone and only the laughter will remain.

What then does this 'healing' amount to? It has not meant our feeling a tiny bit better each day, making perhaps slow but steady progress towards – who knows what? 'Progress', if such it is, is erratic. Our calmer façade can crumble in seconds if ambushed by some unexpected thought or association. Teaching Year 5s about Solomon's Temple being built from the cedars of Lebanon left me almost speechless with a renewed wave of grief at Eddie dying there. Most of the thousand pieces of my shattered mirror may have been carefully replaced, but they are not yet very firmly stuck in. Each one of us has been left a gibbering wreck by something seemingly innocuous. So healing must be seen taking the long view, and recognising that we are coping a little better now than we did six months ago, and twelve months ago, and trusting that we will be doing even better next year. Yet always that tug at our heart-strings, please don't let that be at the cost of our handsome boy slipping from our minds. We love him so much.

Healing has come from hanging on to who we were when Ed was with us and recognising that, beneath the crushing weight of grief, we are still the same. It has come from sharing our sorrow in the family and with those others who loved Ed deeply. It has come from supporting each other. It has come from the prayers of the faithful. It has come from God.

I do not understand why Eddie had to die. I think that Ed's death is the result of a singularly poor piece of divine planning. I cannot imagine what there is to be gained by it. My fevered heart still screams in protest. And yet I believe.

A friend sent me an Easter poem focusing on Mary Magdalene in the garden near Jesus' tomb, who in her distraught state does not recognise Jesus. The poem ends:

'The Word (I AM) Speaks
"Mary"
And her heart is healed.'

I can believe that one day I will hear Jesus' voice say, 'Heather'. The questions, the accusations, the grief, the aching, the void, the 'if only's' – will melt away. All that will remain will be love, joy and – at last – peace. My heart will be healed. It will be finished.

Chapter 12

The Present and the Future

As we live out our third year without our youngest child, where are we now?

In one sense, it is still as though Eddie has never left us. The number of memorials and commemorations has meant that he has seldom been far from the forefront of our minds. His room, although now set up with beds for grandchildren, is and will remain, as the sign on the door still indicates, Edward's room. And, when we are together as a family, we refer to Ed constantly. There seems to be nothing we see or say or think or do, and nowhere we travel, which doesn't make us think of him. We love talking about Ed, and one of our greatest hurts, especially in the early months, was when someone we met – out of fear of upsetting us or from just not having the words to say – acted as though nothing had happened and were unable to mention his name. We have now become more accustomed to making the first move in a conversation to show that it is right and good to talk about him, and once reassured, the vast majority of people have generously responded.

C S Lewis once observed that sorrow is a process, not a state, and that it needs a history, not a map, to chart its course. So we have learned, in part, to manage our sorrow by building a history. Indeed, this narrative, made (as another grieving parent wrote) possible by Ed's life and necessary by his death, has played a crucial part in putting Eddie's life in a historical context.

Our memory of him has developed a sharper focus; our pride in his accomplishments and, above all, in the person he was, is as great as it always was. There is nothing we regret about his upbringing or his life and its living, except that it was more than half a century too short. The 'might have beens' will always remain; and we will now always tend to measure time in terms of before and after Eddie's death. Nevertheless, through the commemorations and many acts of human kindness, and by the mysterious working of God's grace, time has done some of its work.

Perspective

Once time was defined by BC or AD
'Til political correctness changed dates to CE.
These all have lost their importance for me –
Was it before or after Ed died?

1066 is important I'm sure,
Dates of our kings, the commencement of war,
Man on the moon, and so many more
Before Ed died.

But now
The lurch in my heart and catch in my throat
Tell me at once and clearly denote
That a recent event – not one more remote –
Was before or after Ed died.

In this I am certainly not alone;
Parents throughout the ages have known
The different perspective in which time was thrown
When their child died.

(30 January 2007)

As a friend wrote soon after Ed's death: 'We do not think time will actually lessen the sorrow, but through God's peace, time will make it easier to bear'. We have found this to be true and are learning to manage our sorrow. Although the ache of separation still remains, and our lives on earth will always be incomplete until life in all its fullness is accomplished, we have passed beyond the wilderness. A kind of healing has come about through surviving being knocked by the smallest of set-backs, through working through our guilt, and through overcoming our overwhelming tiredness, emptiness and loneliness. Even though the chance discovery of a photograph, the singing of a hymn or a casual comment from a child in class, will trigger a torrent of tears, the waves of grief are less frequent. We now know that we can be happy again.

And we are learning to live and work without self-pity. One measure, among many, of our state of well-being is that we have no need now for (again in C S Lewis' words) the rituals of 'mummification'. We have kept Eddie's birthdays and we visit his grave regularly, but the anniversaries are not wakes, neither is his grave a shrine. Eddie is fondly remembered – I often salute his photograph as I pass it on the landing – but not reverenced. We do not feel the need to keep everything as it was when he was with us for he is always alive in our hearts.

For we firmly believe that Ed, with all the saints, now dwells in the heavenly kingdom (as the prayer for All Saints Sunday puts it), and that he is utterly safe in God's keeping. And until we meet him again in this better world ('the best is what we understand least'), we are learning to remain content with his earthly legacy.

In material and physical terms, this can be precisely measured. He did not leave a will, and apart from about £2,000, an eclectic collection of CDs, some classics and other books, a number of weights, Oxford insignia cricket shirts and a wardrobe of clothes and ties in various stages of decay, his earthly possessions were few. The memorial collections for his charities have raised over £10,000, with the prospect of more to come. Prizes for debating – at Hereford Cathedral School and the Oxford Union – carry his name. And Edward Tomlinson's name is also inscribed on the St Ethelbert memorial in Hereford Cathedral, on a plaque in the Cathedral Sunday School, and on the wooden bench at the sports ground of St John's College, Oxford, as well as on his grave. Ed's photographs continue to adorn our house – not least, at the front of our occasional table for family photographs, where (ironically) he keeps guard over the keys to our garden door. The presidential photograph, from one of his Hilary term 2004 debates, is fixed on the President's staircase at the Oxford Union, where he proudly sits next to Earl Russell, our own former university tutor.

But far more important than these physical reminders are the unseen legacies of Eddie's life on our family, and, we trust, his friends. We are an even closer family, living life more fully and taking nothing for granted. As individuals within that family, we are stronger people, who feel more deeply and are better able to relate to the bereaved of this world, not least those mourning for loved ones who die in war-torn areas. We are also more intensely aware of the frailty of life and can contemplate our own deaths with greater assurance. As John Adams remarked, 'grief drives men to serious reflection, sharpens the understanding and softens the heart.'

And we try to keep Ed's memory alive among our grandchildren who did not know him, by speaking of him and through writing, as in this poem composed, soon after Ed's death, by our son-in-law, Tim Compton. It is entitled 'Your Uncle Ed' and was written for Ollie, Esther and Samuel (and now also for Katy, Reuben and Harriet) 'because we're sure you'll want to know':

Your Uncle Ed

In the beginning ... a cricket-white visitor
Holding NHS curtains at bay.
A carefully chosen bear.
An easy name to say.

Later ... a patient mountain
With newspaper foothills to climb,
A reclining companion viewer
At Wimbledon Final time.

Soon ... those novelty slippers.
A suitcase devoid of shoes.
Two cufflinks and 'hunt-the-tinsel.'
A sporting photo to chew.

Then ... the gap year wake-up calls.
That same familiar bear.
A back-seat dissection of Tacitus.
A litre of milk to share.

Of him we will often remind you
And hope you will remind us some day.
And though it is now hard to find him,
His name will be easy to say.

In these ways, Uncle Eddie's memory will live on, and
perhaps his accomplishments will even influence the lives of
his nephews and nieces. The son of a friend encapsulated
this thought in a wonderful letter of condolence:

> I think it is quite likely that I shared some of your son's experi-
> ences in his time at university – though I only managed to be in
> charge of one of the two equivalent organisations at
> Cambridge! But it is certainly true that there was, for me, a
> strongly affirming effect of 'making it' in the Union, oddly, an
> effect which has recently been more significant for me than it
> was for years after I left university. I also remember that I

The art of spin bowling: some early cricket coaching for nephew
Ollie, Easter 2004

Nephew Ollie and niece Esther gather with the rest of the family
to celebrate their uncles' birthdays, October 2005

admired my uncle, who had been President 30 years before me and that that meant a lot as I made my way through the often tricky world of university politics. The slender consolations that these observations are meant to offer are these: that I know the scale and quality of your son's achievements and can confirm to you that they were most impressive; that they were worth it for him and would have been valuable to him in later life – they were achieved through time well spent; that other young relations really will draw on his inspiration and energy and enjoyment of his time at Oxford.

And for all those who knew him, Eddie's spirit, generosity and laughter are locked in our memories and hearts. Another friend wrote this:

I hope that as you gather together memories of Eddie – photos and writings and talk about him – with the rest of the family, all generations, you will feel drawn closer to him. And being the exceptional person he was, Eddie will be carried 'living on the lips of men' as Virgil wrote of one of his dying heroes – *vivusque per ora feretur.*

It is a fitting epitaph for a remarkable son.

What is love?

What is love, darling Ed, now that you're dead?
Love is yearning, grieving, mourning,
Love is sobbing, sighing, crying,
Love is weeping, wishing, missing,
Love is needing, aching, longing.
Love is in my heart wanting you.

What is love, darling Ed, now that you're dead?
Love is thinking of your childhood,
Love is talking of your antics,
Love is smiling at your photo,
Love is reading through your letters.
Love is in my heart holding you.

What is love, darling Ed, now that you're dead?
Love is sharing recollections,
Love is swapping funny stories,
Love is laughing with your siblings,
Love is wearing your old jumper,
Love is in my heart keeping you.

What is love, darling, Ed, now that you're dead?
Love is quiet, gentle, tender,
Love is honest, truthful, thankful,
Love is trusting, simple, certain.
Love is prayerful, thoughtful, peaceful,
Love is in my heart guarding you.

What is love, darling Ed, now that you're dead?
Love is loving you, Ed,
For our *love* is not dead.

(29 April 2007)